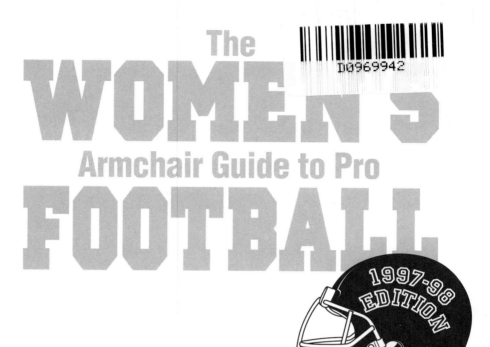

The WOMEN'S
Armchair Guide to Pro
FOOTBALL

1997-98 EDITION

BETSY BERNS

BVision Sportsmedia, L.P., New York, NY

The Women's Armchair Guide to Pro Football

By Betsy Berns

Published by: BVision Sportsmedia, L.P.
                  F.D.R. Station
                  P.O. Box 1176
                  New York, NY 10150-1176

©BVision Sportsmedia, L.P. 1996
©BVision Sportsmedia, L.P. 1997

Library of Congress Catalog Card Number 96-97015

ISBN 0-9653882-1-2

Disclaimer:
The author and publisher have made every effort to ensure accuracy of data, however, there may be typographical or content related errors. This text is intended as a general guide and not as the ultimate football authority. For any discrepancies in information, please refer to the 1996 Official NFL Rule Book and the 1996 NFL Record and Fact Book. In addition, this text contains information as of the printing date; any information occurring after that date is not included in this publication.

This book is intended for entertainment purposes only. Football is not as easy as it looks on TV; therefore, the author and publisher are not liable for any injuries incurred by readers attempting to play professional foot-ball.

The Armchair Guide to Sports series
Armchair Guides are quick, easy, educational, and fun guides to your favorite sports.

DEDICATION

For Doug, my best friend, my inspiration, and my partner for life…
I could never have done this without you.

ACKNOWLEDGMENTS

I can't thank my family enough for all of their love and support. Thank you mom and dad (Barbara and Bert), my new sister Nancy, and of course my three brothers (Adam, Michael, and Dan) for teaching me to love football and for being the greatest friends and brothers in the world. And thanks to my new family, the Korns (Carole, Ron, Karen, Steve and Alissa).

Many wonderful people offered advice and guidance during the writing and publishing phases of this book. My wholehearted thanks goes to all of you, particularly Brent and Andrea Novoselsky, Leigh Steinberg and Jill Peterson, Jeff Gossett, John Frank, and Ronnie Lott. And a big thanks to Vinny Mangano, football coach at Southhampton High School. And of course, thanks to the greatest editor and most exceptional person I know, Doug Korn.

A special thanks goes to Kurt Metzler of Metzler Design for a hall of fame performance in his graphic design, creative ideas, and editorial suggestions.

Thanks for the inspiration, future football fans Jordan, Sarah, Emma and Rachel. In a few years you will be ready to read this.

Graphic Design and Layout: Kurt Metzler

Cover and Author Photos: David Morgan Photography

Cover Football Players: Jim Malone
Jim Lill

Illustrations:
Photos by Archive Photos: p.6, 9, 13, 16, 28, 38, 44, 53, 68, 69, 71, 78, 80, 95, 96, 97
Photos © by Rick Kolodziej: p.19, 61, 65, 66
Photos courtesy of the San Francisco 49ers: p.8, 20, 21, 25, 31, 32, 56, 77
Photos courtesy of the Denver Broncos: p.18, 23, 50, 55, 74
Photos courtesy of the Oakland Raiders: p.20, 29, 37, 38, 75
Photos courtesy of the Miami Dolphins: p.22
Photos courtesy of the Dallas Cowboys: p.23, 31, 76, 77, 78
Photos courtesy of the Detroit Lions: p.23
Photos courtesy of the Green Bay Packers: p.24, 28, 58
Photos courtesy of the Chicago Bears: p.24, 29, 30, 43, 57, 67, 68
Photos courtesy of the Buffalo Bills: p.30
Photos courtesy of the New York Jets: p. 71, 76, 94
Photo courtesy of Steinberg & Moorad: p. 83
Photos courtesy of Vernon J. Biever (Green Bay Packers): p. 58, 70
Photos courtesy of Ronnie Lott: p. 32, 91

NFL Team helmets courtesy of the National Football League, Properties Inc.

TABLE OF CONTENTS

PREFACE:

Football is for Women Too!

Do you lose your boyfriend, husband, and/or friends to the sport of football for five months out of the year? Do you find yourself left out of conversations about football, because you can't follow what your friends or co-workers are talking about? Do you ever try to watch a football game and lose interest because you don't understand the rules of the game? If you answer yes to any of these questions, you are not alone. Most American women answer yes to one of these questions. Unlike men, few women today grew up playing organized football or even playing touch football with friends. Until now there has not been a fun and easy way for women to learn about the game.

The Women's Armchair Guide to Pro Football was written to change all that.

You'll soon realize why football has become America's most popular sport, and why football legends, such as "Broadway" Joe Namath, Dan Marino, and Joe Montana, have become important icons in American culture. You'll also understand why millions of American males are glued to their seats each weekend. Football is a real life soap opera, complete with old-fashioned rivalries, outstanding athletic feats and heart-warming failures, quirky personalities, extraordinary leadership and teamwork and, of course, exorbitant sums of money.

Watching and enjoying football requires learning the basics and nuances of the sport. *The Women's Armchair Guide To Pro Football* will teach you all you need to know in order to watch, understand and enjoy a professional football game.

Football is a fun game, so a book about football should be fun. This book explores the lighter side of the game as well as the intensity of competition. You will find that this book is not overly technical, so you don't have to know anything about football when you pick it up.

The Women's Armchair Guide To Pro Football is packed with "Fun Facts" and "Helpful Hints" which relate interesting trivia, stories of great accomplishment, and useful concepts to keep in mind. For easy reference, there is a list of important "takeaway" points at the end of each chapter, as well as a glossary of terms at the end of the book.

The book is divided into four quarters, like a football game. When you get to halftime, you can pat yourself on the back. At that point, you've learned the basics and are ready to move on to more advanced topics.

In short, you'll soon learn all about football in less time than it takes to watch a professional game. So sit back in a comfortable chair, relax, and get ready to follow the game like a pro.

WELCOME TO THE GAME

Welcome to **The Women's Armchair Guide to Pro Football.** This book is meant to be educational, but just as importantly, it is meant to be fun. Read this book at your own pace. Skip around if you want. When things get a little technical, take a break and read a fun fact or two.

The book is designed for readers with all levels of knowledge about football. If you know nothing about football, this book will teach you how to watch, enjoy, and follow the game. If you already know a little about football, some parts may seem obvious to you, but keep going. You'll be surprised what you will learn. There's more to football than meets the eye.

The first quarter will explain the fundamentals of the game. The first two chapters will introduce you to the basics of football, such as scoring, offense and defense, downs, and the clock. The next two chapters go into more detail on offense and defense, including the various positions and responsibilities. The concepts you learn will be used throughout the rest of the book.

The second quarter is a mix of fundamentals and famous football stories. You'll learn about special teams, which come on the field at designated points of the game. You'll be introduced to the playing field plus key rules and penalties. To lighten things up, the quarter ends with a description of some of the most triumphant, and embarrassing, moments in the history of the NFL.

Halftime in a football game is a chance for a team to catch its breath and regroup for the second half. In the halftime section of this book, you'll go behind the scenes to get a glimpse of the hard work demanded of a typical NFL player in an ordinary week. Football, as you'll see, isn't all touchdowns and glory.

The third quarter will teach you how to watch the game and enhance your viewing experience. You'll read about how football evolved from an Ivy League experiment into the high stakes drama it is today. This section also takes you off the field for an exclusive interview with super-agent Leigh Steinberg and for snapshots of the college draft process and the pre-season.

The fourth quarter is the most advanced section of the book. Included you will find illustrations of penalties and you will learn about the two conferences and six divisions that make up the NFL plus the post-season road to the Championship. By the time you've completed the fourth quarter, you'll feel like you've been watching the game for years.

Read on and enjoy.

TRAINING CAMP (THE BASICS)

A game of territory...

Football is a game of territory. Like two armies doing battle, each team is assigned territory to defend against the other team. Each team tries to advance (with possession of the ball) towards the opponent's territory. You can also think of football as a life-sized chess game filled with strategy and cunning and, of course, over-sized men running into each other at full force.

A game consists of two opposing teams taking turns trying to score points when they have possession of the ball. The team with the most points when the game clock runs out wins the game.

Each team has three squads of players: **offense, defense,** and **special teams.** Players are typically assigned to offense or defense, and many are also assigned to one or more of the special teams.

A football game is divided into **plays.** A play starts when the ball is hiked and lasts until a referee signals that the play is over by blowing a whistle. In between plays, the teammates take a brief break to regroup and get ready for the next play.

FUN FACT

Football is the most popular professional sport in America. During the 1995-1996 season, an average 113 million Americans watched NFL football each weekend. Super Bowl XXX, in January 1996, was seen by over 138 million in the U.S. Through the end of the 1995-1996 season, seven of the top ten American TV audiences of all time were for Super Bowls.

Offense and defense...

The two teams alternate playing offense and defense. The team which starts the play with the ball is called the **offense.** The offense tries to advance the ball in order to score points. The **defense** is the squad of players trying to prevent the offense from advancing and scoring. If the offense fails to advance the ball by ten yards within four plays (more detail on this comes later), the ball is turned over to the other team, which then goes on offense. Another way for the defensive team to regain possession of the ball is to take the ball away on a play through a **fumble** recovery or an **interception,** each also called a **turnover.** (See explanations later in the book.)

Each team, offense and defense, is allowed to have eleven players on the field at once. A team that has more than eleven players on the field during a play will be punished by the referees. Punishment in football comes in the form of a **penalty.** There are many ways to incur a penalty in football, some of which you will learn about in Chapter Seven, Rules of the Game. If a team is careless enough to have fewer than eleven players on the field for a play, there is no penalty but the team's players will be outnumbered and at a disadvantage.

Referee signalling a face mask penalty.

During his brief stint as a 49er, "Neon" Deion Sanders teaches quarterback Steve Young how to do a celebration dance.

FUN FACT

In modern football, positions have become so specialized that very few players play both offense and defense. However, Deion Sanders (currently with the Dallas Cowboys) is one of the fastest and most athletic players in the game. A star defensive back at the cornerback position, he also returns kicks on special teams and is used from time to time on the offense as a pass receiver. Until recently, Sanders also played major league baseball as an outfielder for the Atlanta Braves and Cincinnati Reds. Sanders earned the nicknames "Prime Time" for his clutch performances and colorful celebrations and "Neon" Deion for his flashy style.

A method to the madness...

From the novice viewer's standpoint, football probably seems very disorganized. However, the players on the field begin each play with a detailed plan of action designed to advance the ball on offense or prevent its advancement on defense. Each team tries to anticipate the opponent's strategy to tailor its plans to the opponent and to the situation in the game. The plays have been drilled into the players' minds and bodies in practice. Coaches and players spend endless hours mapping out plays and strategizing how to outwit and outperform the other team. When you read Chapter Nine, A Week in the Life of a Professional Player, you will be surprised to see how much time a football player spends in strategy meetings.

Sometimes these well-laid plans work like clockwork, and other times they fail miserably.

FUN FACT

Over Nineteen million people attended NFL football games during the 1995-1996 season, including the pre-season and the playoffs. This was an all-time record, with average paid attendance per game exceeding 60,000.

Knowing the score...

When a team's offensive squad is on the field, its ultimate goal is to score a **touchdown.** A touchdown is scored when a team crosses the opponent's **goal line** with the ball. A touchdown is worth six points to the scoring team. Importantly, a team which scores a touchdown automatically gets an extra scoring opportunity worth one or two extra points. Most of the time, the team will kick the ball through the **goalposts,** which is worth one extra point, and commonly called the **extra point attempt, point after touchdown,** or **conversion.** The team's other choice is to run or pass the ball into the end zone, which is worth two points and is commonly called a **two point conversion attempt.**

The offensive team can earn points without scoring a touchdown by kicking a **field goal,** which is worth three points to the scoring team. A field goal occurs when the offensive team kicks the football through the opposing team's goalposts. Field goals and the reason for choosing the field goal option are explained in more detail in Chapter Five, The "Special" Ones.

HELPFUL HINT

Remember, the most points a team can score on one play is six points for a touchdown. Immediately after the celebration surrounding the touchdown (dancing, hugging, slapping hands) has subsided, the scoring team has an extra point opportunity. If that team takes the riskier route and throws or runs the ball into the end zone, they can earn two points, for a total of eight points. If they kick the ball through the goal posts, they will get only one extra point, for a total of seven. However, by kicking the ball, the team is more likely to succeed and get this extra point, so most of the time the team will elect to play it safe and kick. A team only gets one try on an extra point attempt. A failed attempt brings no extra points.

FUN FACT

Joe Montana, star quarterback of the San Francisco 49ers, was known for his leadership and calm temperament under fire. In Super Bowl XXIII in Miami in 1989, the 49ers were down 16-13 against the Cincinnati Bengals late in the game and had the ball on their own eight yard line, 92 yards away from a touchdown. Sensing that his team was feeling the pressure of the situation, Montana spotted comedian John Candy in the audience and pointed him out to tackle Harris Barton in the 49er huddle. The antic helped to loosen up the 49er offense, which proceeded to march down the field and score a touchdown on a Montana pass to John Taylor. With a successful extra point attempt, the 49ers pulled out a 20-16 victory.

Joe Montana

First and ten...

A series of offensive plays in football is divided into **downs.** The offensive team gets four plays (or four downs) to move the ball forward ten yards. When the offense starts a series with the ball, it is called first down. The second play is called second down, and so on. Each time the offense moves the ball forward by the required ten yards, the counting of downs becomes reset at first down, giving the offense four more plays to advance the ball. The offense must continue to earn first downs or score, or it must give up possession of the football to the other team.

Turning it over...

The offensive series of plays continues until the offense:
1. fails to pick up the required ten yards within four plays and turns the ball over to the opposing team;
2. scores a touchdown;
3. turns the ball over to the other team on an interception or fumble (see Chapter Four, The Defenders); or
4. kicks the ball, either as a punt or field goal attempt. (See Chapter Two, Getting in Shape.)

FUN FACT

Some pro football stars have gone on to illustrious careers in public service. Byron "Whizzer" White was a star running back for Pittsburgh in the 1930's, leading the league in rushing in 1938. White later served as a justice on the U.S. Supreme Court. Jack Kemp, star quarterback for the AFC champion Buffalo Bills in the 1960's, became a U.S. congressman, Housing Secretary, and 1996 Republican vice presidential candidate.

Jack Kemp

HELPFUL HINT

The offense has different strategies for each down depending on the distance required for a first down and the status of the game. This makes sense; if you are on your first attempt at performing a task, and you know you have three more attempts left, you will approach the task differently than you would if you knew it was your final try. More on different offensive strategies appears in Chapter Three, The Aggressors. The defense tailors its strategy based on what it expects from the offense and how much yardage can be given up without allowing a first down.

Turning the ball over to the opposing team is, of course, distasteful to the offense, since it means giving the opponent a scoring opportunity. When turning the ball over seems imminent because getting a first down looks unlikely, the offense wants the other team to advance the ball as far down the field (as far away from the offense's goal line) as possible. In this case, on fourth down the team with the ball will most likely elect to **punt** the ball down the field rather than trying for a long-shot first down.

When possession of the ball changes from one team to the other, the defensive and the offensive squads switch. If Atlanta's offense gives up the ball to Detroit's defense, then Atlanta's defense comes on the field to defend against Detroit's offensive squad.

The Clock is ticking...

Just as this book is divided into four sections, a game of football is divided into four quarters of fifteen minutes each. The game is tracked on a clock, referred to as the **game clock,** which shows the time remaining in a given quarter. There is a twelve minute intermission called **halftime** between the second and third quarters. Those of you who have watched a full game of football know the game lasts much longer than an hour. A typical game lasts about three hours from beginning to end. This is because the game clock is stopped constantly — after certain types of plays (an incomplete pass or when a player with the ball steps out of bounds), when a player is injured, when a penalty is called, when a team takes a brief break to discuss strategy with its coaches (a **time out**), and between quarters.

Sometimes you will notice that the game stops for no apparent reason; this probably means that the TV network

HELPFUL HINT

While football is a game of territory, the territory each team defends alternates each quarter. This is to eliminate any advantage which a particular side of the field might bring on a given day, such as having the wind at a team's back, or any disadvantage like facing into the sun. At the end of each quarter, the teams switch sides of the field and each defends the opposite end.

HELPFUL HINT

The first team that scores in overtime (any type of scoring counts) wins the game. This extended playing time (overtime) is also called **sudden death.** It can feel like sudden death if your team unexpectedly loses an important game. Overtime can also feel like *slow* death if you happen to be watching an unexciting game that seems to be going on forever.

broadcasting the game has required a break for a commercial. Somebody has to help pay all those multi-million dollar player salaries.

If the fourth quarter ends in a tie, play will continue in **overtime** until one team scores. During the regular season, overtime is limited to one extra fifteen minute period. If the score is still tied after this overtime period, the game is over and declared a tie.

In the **post-season** (during the **playoffs** and the **Super Bowl**) there are no ties, so the game goes on indefinitely until one team scores to win.

FUN FACT

The longest pro football game in NFL history, lasting more than 82 minutes, was played in 1971. In a divisional playoff game with the Miami Dolphins visiting the Kansas City Chiefs, the game was tied 24-24 after the four regulation quarters. In the first overtime quarter, neither team managed to score. Seven minutes and 40 seconds into the second overtime quarter, Garo Yepremian (a former soccer player from Cyprus) won the game for Miami when he kicked a 37-yard field goal giving Miami a 27-24 victory. Yepremian also became immortalized in football history for his ill-fated 1973 pass attempt described as "The Pass" in Chapter Eight, NFL Memorable Moments.

Remember:

- The offense is the team with the ball, trying to score points.

- The defense is the team without the ball, trying to prevent the offense from scoring points.

- Each team is allowed to have eleven players on the field at once.

- The offensive team is allowed four tries, or downs, to move the ball forward ten yards.

- The game is divided into four quarters of fifteen minutes each.

- In overtime, the first team to score wins the game. •

GETTING IN SHAPE
(More Basic Knowledge)

Now that you have a general idea of what the game is all about, we'll move on to more of the basics. If you come across a word you don't understand, look it up in the glossary.

FUN FACT

Football is a sport that evolved out of two kicking games — soccer and rugby. Professional style tackle football is typically played with helmets and protective padding. Less violent variations of football have been developed for less serious games. Variations include touch football (instead of tackling, the play ends when an opposing player touches the player with the ball) and flag football (players wear detachable cloth straps at their waist, and the play ends when a player with the ball has one of his "flags" removed).

The Huddle...

In between plays, the offensive and defensive players on the field gather together to discuss their strategies for the next play. Each team forms a small circle called the **huddle.**

HELPFUL HINT

A football team uses only one of its squads at a time. For example, a team's offense and defense are not on the field at the same time. Most players belong to either the offensive or defensive squad. It is rare for a player to play on both, however frequently a player will play on either the offense or defense and then also play for one of the special kicking situation teams.

HELPFUL HINT

The line of scrimmage is where the ball sits at the beginning of a play. If the Tampa Bay Buccaneers have the ball, and it is second down and seven (yards to go) from their own 35, the line of scrimmage is the 35-yard line. If the Buccaneers try a forward pass which is incomplete, the ball returns to the same line of scrimmage, the 35-yard line. If the pass is completed, the line of scrimmage for the next play moves to where the pass receiver is tackled.

See Chapter Eight: NFL Memorable Momemts for more on the 1970's Pittsburgh Steelers.

The offensive huddle takes place behind the line of scrimmage, so that the defense cannot hear what is being said. In the offensive huddle, the quarterback informs the team of the next play. The plays have typically been memorized by the offense in advance, so each player knows from the play selected who will get the ball and what each player's role is during the play.

In the defensive huddle, a player such as the defensive captain is assigned to explain the strategy for the next play.

The line of scrimmage...

After each play, the referees have the responsibility for placing the ball on the field with its ends pointing toward the opposing goal lines. The ball is placed at the yard line where the last play ended. There is some judgment involved in accurately placing **(spotting)** the ball, and sometimes players and fans complain about a supposed bad **spot** (placement) which favors the other team. In general though, professional referees are pretty good at spotting the ball.

When the players line up against each other, there is an imaginary line separating them called the **line of scrimmage.** This imaginary line runs sideways from the ball to the sidelines. The area between the opposing linemen is called the **neutral zone** and is off-limits before the play springs into action beginning with the snapping of the ball. Even though they're behind the line, offensive linemen are not allowed to move toward the line of scrimmage until the ball is put in play. The offense controls when the play starts and, by moving, could falsely signal the defense that the play has begun.

FUN FACT

Defensive players in the NFL have traditionally had colorful nicknames. The Minnesota Vikings defensive line in the 1970's was known as the Purple People Eaters. "Mean" Joe Greene of the 1970's era Pittsburgh Steelers was part of the team's "Steel Curtain" defense. Ed "Too Tall" Jones, standing 6'9" and weighing 287 lbs., played defense for the Dallas Cowboys in the 1980's.

As you've heard, the offense has four plays to move the ball ten yards or more or to score. If the offense is successful in moving the ball ten yards, the offensive team gets to keep the ball. Otherwise, the offense loses possession of the ball to the other team. The progress of the offense is measured by the distance the ball moves down the field during its possession.

Decision time – what to do on fourth down...

For reasons that may be apparent to you by now, the fourth down is a critical decision point for the offense. The coach of the offense has three choices.

The offense can try for a first down or a touchdown. If the offense gets the required yardage for a first down, the offense gets to retain the ball. If the offense comes up short, the defense takes over the ball. "Going for it" on fourth down, although usually popular with the fans, is often risky. Most fourth downs result in a kick – either a field goal attempt or a punt.

FUN FACT

George Blanda, the Energizer Bunny™ of the NFL, played in the league during four decades (1949-1975) and holds many league records. Blanda played the most seasons (26) and games (340) of any NFL player. Blanda, a place kicker and a quarterback, holds the NFL career scoring record with 2002 points and extra point record with 943 points. In his final season, Blanda (at age 48) played against players who had not yet been born when he entered the league.

George Blanda

A field goal is worth three points, and the coach must assess the probability of success on the field goal versus the probability of getting a first down and retaining possession of the ball. (Remember, retaining possession of the ball keeps the possibility of a touchdown alive.) The field position of the ball, the score of the game, and the time remaining on the clock each factor heavily into a decision regarding a field goal attempt. Depending on the kicker and the playing conditions, such as the wind, the offense usually needs to be inside the defense's 20- to 30-yard lines to have a high likelihood of success. After a missed field goal, the defense takes over the ball at the previous line of scrimmage or the 20-yard line.

See
**Chapter Three:
The Aggressors**
(Time Out section)
for a further explanation
and some examples of a
series of downs.

See Chapter Three: The Aggressors (Time Out section) for a further explanation and some examples of a series of downs.

FUN FACT

Football players today wear jerseys and pants that fit
tightly, making it more difficult for their opponents to
grab their clothing to help bring them to the ground.
Some players even go as far as sewing velcro tape
on the inside of their uniforms to help the material
stick closer to their skin and pads.

HELPFUL HINT

You should not con-
fuse the scoring term
safety with the defen-
sive player called the
safety. Although the
same term is used, it
means two different
things. Listen for the
way the word is used
in a sentence
and you will
know
whether
the
term
refers
to a
play or
a player.

*Referee
signalling
safety*

On a fourth down play, if the offensive players are not
within field goal range they have another option. The
offense can **punt** (or **drop-kick**) the ball down the field,
turning it over to the defense further down the field.
Now, when the opponent takes over on offense, the
opponent should have further to go in order to score.
There is no assurance how far the punt will travel, however, and the other team has the opportunity to block or run
back the punt. Punting is explained in detail in Chapter
Five, The "Special" Ones.

FUN FACT

A typical football game lasts approximately three
hours. In those three hours there will be on average
four or five touchdowns, a few field goals and
around 100 plays. In a soccer game, the scoring is
less frequent. An exciting soccer game may end with
a 1-0 or maybe a 2-1 score. It's no wonder that
football is growing in popularity worldwide.

As you can see, each of these fourth down options
involve risks and trade-offs. Fans and sportscasters can be
relentless in criticizing a coach if he makes what turns out
to be a wrong decision on a crucial fourth down play.
Some people call this Monday morning quarterbacking.
Understanding what the offense chooses to do in various
fourth down situations is complicated, but it is an important part of understanding and enjoying the game.

The Safety...

The only other form of scoring in football which has not
yet been discussed is the **safety,** a relatively rare form of
scoring by the defense. A safety typically occurs when a
defensive player tackles an offensive player with the ball in
the offensive player's own end zone. A safety is worth two

points to the defending team. Following a safety, the team which scores the two points also gets the ball back (after a kick by the other team called a free kick). This is the only time in football that the team which scores also gets the ball back.

Types of scoring, a review...

At this point, it is useful to review the different ways a team can score and the number of points assigned to each scoring situation. See the chart below for an outline of the different ways to score points.

TYPES OF SCORING

Touchdown (6 points)	Extra Point (1 or 2 points)	Field Goal (3 points)	Safety (2 points)
A team scores a touchdown by either running the ball over the opponent's goal line into the end zone or completing a pass to a player in the end zone.	After a touchdown, a team can either kick the ball through the goal posts for one extra point or run or pass the ball into the end zone for two points. The scoring team gets one try, and the choice to go for one or two points is up to the scoring team's coach.	A field goal is made by kicking the ball over the crossbar and between the goal posts. If the ball fails to go through the goal posts, the kicking team will not get three points and the defensive team will take possession of the ball. Field goal attempts are usually made on fourth down.	The play where the defense scores points. This is accomplished when the offensive team gets trapped in its own end zone. The defensive team gets a bonus of two points and gets to receive the ball back on a free kick.

Substituting players...

Free substitution (substitution of players without any limits on the number or frequency) was introduced during World War II out of necessity, permanently changing the game. When the younger players were drafted, the older men who took their place had a hard time playing a full game. Free substitution was born, allowing players to rest while others took their place on the field. This change led coaches to recognize the strategic advantage of using specialists. Substituting players makes sense, since the same type of athlete that excels at throwing or kicking the ball may not be much of a blocker or tackler.

If a player is tired, hurt or just not playing well, the coach is allowed to substitute another player at his position at any point in the game. Sometimes a coach substitutes a

Referee signalling touchdown

player into the game for a given role on a specific play. For example, a coach may substitute extra pass receivers for running backs in a passing situation. Substitutions can only be made between plays. Once a play has begun, there are no substitutions until the play is over.

Remember:

- The offense is permitted four tries to run or pass the ball for a total of ten yards. If the offense fails to gain the required ten yards, the ball is turned over to the other team.

- If a team succeeds at advancing the ball over the opponent's goal line, this is a touchdown and the scoring team gets six points.

- After a touchdown, a team can either kick the ball through the goal posts for an extra point or run or pass the ball into the end zone for two points.

- On fourth down, the coach of the offensive team has three options: 1) try for a first down; 2) attempt to kick a field goal; or 3) punt.

- A safety is scored when a defensive player traps an offensive ball carrier in the offensive team's end zone. •

Boomer Esiason (Cincinnati Bengals), Eric Dickerson (L.A. Raiders), Phil Simms (N.Y. Giants), Howie Long (L.A. Raiders), Lawrence Taylor (N.Y. Giants), and John Elway (Denver Broncos) were made to appear bald for a television potato chip commercial that ran during the 1993 Super Bowl. The players were supposed to have shaved their heads after losing a bet.

THE AGGRESSORS

Introduction to the offense...

The offense is the team with possession of the ball at the beginning of a play. The offensive team (you may not find them offensive, but that's another way this squad is described) is made up of the quarterback and a mix of linemen, receivers, backs, and tight ends. As you will recall, the offense is made up of eleven players on the field at a time. However, the coach of the offensive team has some flexibility in how he configures his players. A typical configuration is five interior linemen (two guards, one center, two tackles), two receivers, two backs, one tight end and one quarterback arranged as shown here:

The Offensive linemen...

Offensive linemen line up at the line of scrimmage. The man at the center of the offensive line is called the **center.** (So far this is not very difficult.) The center is the first player on the offensive team to touch the ball. He bends over the ball, which is lying on the ground, and **snaps** it (hands it or throws it back between his legs) to the quarterback to begin the play.

The snap is also referred to as hiking the ball. A play begins when the center lifts the ball off of the

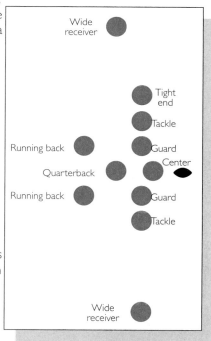

Gary Zimmerman
Offensive Tackle
Denver Broncos

ground. This is the signal to the offensive and defensive players that they can start the play. For the linemen, it means they can start crashing into each other. If a player on either team moves too early or crosses the line of scrimmage before the ball is snapped, a penalty can be called on that player's team.

The **quarterback** is the focus of the offensive team, responsible for throwing, handing off or running with the ball, so he needs as much protection as possible. Most of the quarterback's job involves getting the ball into the hands of other players on a running or a passing play. If he does not have enough time to execute the play, it is unlikely the ball will advance. For this reason, there are many people on the field assigned to protecting the quarterback.

After the center snaps the ball, he then refocuses on **blocking** the defensive linemen across from him to protect, or clear a space for, the man with the ball. Snapping the ball back consistently is not as easy as it sounds. If the center snaps the ball back too low, too high, or too wide, the quarterback may drop it or find himself off balance and perhaps out of position. When the play begins, every fraction of a second counts.

The linemen on either side of the center join the center in guarding the quarterback. These two players are called, appropriately, **guards.** The guards try to push off (block) the defensive linemen in order to protect the quarterback and give him as much time as possible to find his target for advancing the ball.

In addition to the center and two guards, there are two more players who block for the quarterback. They are called **tackles.** The tackles line up outside the two guards. Oddly enough, the rules have changed over the years, and offensive tackles are no longer allowed to do any tackling. They are only allowed to block for the quarterback or block for other offensive players who have the ball.

Despite the importance of their roles, the offensive linemen are often the least recognized players on a team. They rarely handle the ball once it's in play, so you don't see them throwing or catching touchdown passes. For the most part, you will hear an offensive lineman's name mentioned when he has done something wrong, such as being called for a holding penalty or offsides.

Offensive linemen should possess size, strength, and speed to be able to block effectively. In addition to being big and powerful, good linemen should also be intelligent. The best offensive linemen don't just stand there and rely on their size, strength and speed to protect the quarterback. They watch the defense closely to try and react to the defense's strategy and movement.

FUN FACT

Offensive linemen in the NFL have been getting bigger and bigger over the years. The average weight for the starting offensive line of the of the Dallas Cowboys in 1996 was approximately 315 lbs. Compare this to the Cleveland Browns' 1982 offensive linemen who were required to weigh less than 260 lbs.

HELPFUL HINT

Offensive linemen are not allowed to use their hands to hold the defensive players while blocking. If one is caught doing so, he incurs a holding penalty.

Offensive linemen are not allowed to catch a pass. This is because it is not practical for the defense to defend

FUN FACT

In recent years, a pre-game ritual for the offensive linemen of the Minnesota Vikings was to show up four hours before game time, dress for the game, and sit in the team locker room around a cooler of Mountain Dew, consuming cups of the green beverage until the rest of the team arrived.

One season, the wife of Vikings kicker Rich Karlis made the mistake of referring to the team's offensive linemen as a "bunch of slobs". The linemen punished Karlis for his wife's comment by stringing him up from the goal posts. You can bet no one on the team ever disparaged this group again.

against all ten players besides the quarterback on a passing play. If the defense had to cover the offensive linemen on passing plays, there would be no players available to rush the quarterback. In football terms, we say that the offensive linemen are **ineligible receivers.** If an offensive lineman does catch a pass, the play does not count and a penalty is called.

A team's success is closely tied to the quality of its offensive line. If

Jeff Hostetler
Quarterback
Oakland Raiders

the offensive line doesn't protect the quarterback, the quarterback can't do his job. If the quarterback can't do his job, then the wide receivers, running backs, and tight end can't do their jobs. As you can see, the role of the offensive line is very important. Perhaps for this reason, and because these oversized players often feel unrecognized or underappreciated, a pro team's offensive line is often a very tight knit and proud group of men, often demonstrating quirky, colorful personalities.

The Quarterback...

The **quarterback** is the most visible, and often the most glamorous, player on the team. He directs the team before and during a play, much like an army general. Like a general in the midst of battle, it is crucial that the quarterback remain poised amidst the tumult. He can't get rattled or let his concentration be thrown off during the game. The quarterback is often either revered or blamed, depending on his and the team's performance, and the outcome of the game.

Joe Montana
Quarterback
San Francisco 49ers

FUN FACT

Even with all of the pressure that they endure, many quarterbacks retain a playful side. Joe Montana, star quarterback of the San Francisco 49ers (1979-1992) and Kansas City Chiefs (1993-1994) is considered by many to be one of the best all-around quarterbacks in history. Montana led his team to four Super Bowl victories. However, Montana was a practical joker. He was known for stealing his teammates' bikes after practice and hiding them in trees.

The offense has to know the opposing defense well to call effective plays. Some quarterbacks (especially those who have been playing pro football for a number of years) call many of their own plays, while most rely on their coaches to signal the plays from the sidelines.

Once the quarterback has called the play in the **huddle,** he and his teammates go back to the **line of scrimmage** prepared to carry out their new set of orders. The quarterback lines up behind the center in order to take possession of the ball to start off an offensive play. To officially start the new play, the quarterback will call out a series of **signals** to his team, which is also known as the **count.**

The signals are in a pre-arranged code that should only be meaningful to the offense.

The signals will be short words screamed in a peculiar code, such as "blue 42, hut, hut, hut". As odd as this sounds, the quarterback's teammates will know what this means. For example, he may have told his team, in the huddle, that the ball will be snapped on the second "hut" sound. Since the offense knows when the ball is supposed to be snapped, it should have a split second advantage in getting started. If the center makes a mistake, however, and snaps the ball on the third "hut", you may see the peculiar sight of a whole offense moving before the play has started. Needless to say, this will result in a penalty.

Sometimes the quarterback will use this code to indicate to his teammates that he is changing the play from what he called in the huddle to something new. Perhaps he sees something in the defense's formation that indicates to him that the initial play will not work. This switch at the last minute is termed calling an **audible,** since he is audibly changing the play at the line of scrimmage. Calling an audible is like changing your order in a restaurant when you see something that looks better at the next table.

Sometimes the home team's fans will try to make as much noise as possible to prevent a visiting offensive team from hearing the count. This is one of the factors that contributes to what is often termed home field advantage.

HELPFUL HINT

Try to familiarize yourself with the names of the starting quarterbacks for your favorite teams. Quarterbacks are constantly in the media so it shouldn't be that difficult. For names of some current quarterbacks for the 1997 football season, refer to Chapter Seventeen, The Conferences, NFC and AFC Teams, Profiles and Personalities.

FUN FACT

Some players excel at quarterback because of their speed and ability to avoid tackles. Steve Young, the quarterback for the San Francisco 49ers, is known as one of the best running quarterbacks in the NFL. He will often keep the ball himself and run to gain yardage when he cannot find an open pass receiver. Young is also a solid passer, however. He threw for six touchdowns without a single interception during Super Bowl XXIX.

Steve Young
Quarterback
San Francisco 49ers

When the play begins, the quarterback will take the ball from the center and hand it to one of the running backs, throw a pass to a wide receiver or a tight end, or keep the ball and run it himself. Sometimes the original play called does not work, and the quarterback is forced to improvise.

Dan Marino
Quarterback
Miami Dolphins

FUN FACT

Some quarterbacks are great at passing, but can't run very well. The best example of this is Dan Marino, star quarterback for the Miami Dolphins since 1983. Marino holds four of the NFL's most important career passing records (attempts, completions, yardage and touchdowns). As you watch him play, however, you will notice that Marino rarely runs with the ball. He has suffered from leg injuries and has limited mobility.

At times, fans confuse celebrity status in football with celebrity status in the movies. One Sunday afternoon, while watching an NFL game on TV, a female observer heard her friends cheer for Dan Marino. She glanced at the TV and remarked, "I didn't think Dan Marino was a real person, I just thought he was a character in [the movie] *Ace Ventura, Pet Detective*". In fact, the real Dan Marino played himself in that hit comedy.

See Chapter Twelve: The Draft for more on Dan Marino.

Running backs...

Running backs start in the back of the offense and are expected to run with the football on most running plays, thus the name. They line up behind the quarterback, in an area called the **offensive backfield.** Running backs will not necessarily stand directly behind the quarterback, but may line up on his left or right side. They are positioned to be able to pick up running momentum before the quarterback hands them the football.

Once he has the ball, a running back looks for holes (openings where there are no tacklers) in the defense to run through. A running back has to be quick and tough, with extremely powerful legs to help force his way through the defense and gain extra yardage after being hit by a defensive player. An active running back may be tackled ten to twenty times or more during the course of a game, mostly by players who are bigger than he is, and sometimes by many players at once. It is not surprising that running backs are highly susceptible to injuries.

Versatile running backs can be used for more than just running plays. The running back is an **eligible receiver,** so he can catch passes thrown by the quarterback.

FUN FACT

Emmitt Smith of the Dallas Cowboys is considered by many to be one of the finest running backs in football today. Smith's star performances helped the Cowboys win Super Bowls in the 1992, 1993 and 1995 seasons. Due to Smith's speed (he accelerates with unusual quickness), strength (his thighs look like tree trunks), and his proximity to the ground (he is only 5'9"tall), Smith is extremely difficult to tackle.

Emmitt Smith
Running Back
Dallas Cowboys

Running backs are also referred to as backs, **fullbacks, and halfbacks,** largely based upon where they line up for the play. A team typically lines up with one or two running backs. On a passing play, the running backs may have the added responsibility of blocking for the quarterback, forming a second layer of protection against defensive linemen who get past the offensive line.

FUN FACT

Barry Sanders, a running back for the Detroit Lions since 1989, is one of the most exciting running backs in the NFL. At 5'8" and weighing 200 lbs., Sanders possesses unusual speed and balance with a startling combination of power and agility. He, at times, looks like a dancer as he darts in and out of his opponents' way.

Barry Sanders
Running Back
Detroit Lions

Tight end...

A player at the end of the offensive line, lined up just outside a tackle, is called the **tight end.** He gets his name because he is lined up tightly next to the offensive line, on the end of the line. The most common formation uses one tight end, although teams sometimes use two.

The tight end has many of the same blocking responsibilities as other members of the offensive line; the difference is that the tight end has an additional responsibility. He is **eligible** to catch passes thrown by the quarterback. A tight end, therefore, must possess size and strength to block, but also speed and pass-catching ability to act as a receiver.

Shannon Sharpe
Tight End
Denver Broncos

FUN FACT

According to John Frank (former tight end for the San Francisco 49ers, 1984-1988), tight ends are "a mixture between bulky linemen and graceful wide receivers. The best tight ends capitalize on both. (Tight ends) are similar in size and agility to linebackers" says Frank, (see Chapter Four, The Defenders) "but with a different, less mean disposition." According to Frank, "If somebody of that size and speed can't catch, then he has to develop a nasty disposition and become a linebacker." John Frank, known in his football playing days as a fiercely competitive and intelligent player, left the 49ers after four seasons to pursue his dream of becoming a doctor. He is currently in residency at Loyola Medical School as an ear, nose, and throat specialist.

Mark Chmura
Tight End
Green Bay Packers

Sometimes people may refer to tight ends as, simply, ends. In the next chapter you will learn that the defensive squad also has a position that is referred to as an end (defensive end). If you remember that a tight end plays on offense and the other type of end plays on defense, you should be able to keep them straight.

FUN FACT

One of the most intense tight ends to play pro football was Mike Ditka. In 1961, while playing for the Chicago Bears, Ditka became Rookie of the Year by scoring twelve touchdowns and catching passes for more than 1,000 yards. After his football playing career ended, Ditka went on to coach the Chicago Bears for eleven years. Ditka's aggressive coaching style and blunt personality have become legendary. *Saturday Night Live* made fun of Ditka's popularity and personality in a recurring skit known as "Da Bears".

Mike Ditka
Tight End & later Head Coach
Chicago Bears

Wide receivers...

The two **wide receivers** (also called **pass receivers,** or just **receivers**) are stationed off to either side of the offensive line. Their job is to receive passes, thus the name. Receivers are the offensive players closest to the sidelines, which is what the term "wide" describes. The wide receiver's job is to run down field (called running a pass **pattern**) and catch the ball when the quarterback throws it to him. Once he has caught the ball, the receiver's job is to run with the ball as far as he can go without getting tackled. The receiver is often the "speedster" of the offensive squad. In fact, some stars of track and field have gone on to excel as NFL receivers.

FUN FACT

Jerry Rice, star wide receiver for the San Francisco 49ers since 1985, broke three Super Bowl records (for most career touchdowns, points, and receiving yards) in Super Bowl XXIX. He is generally considered the best wide receiver to have ever played the game. Rice possesses an exceptional work ethic. Despite having little left to prove, he trains harder and longer (than some believe is humanly possible) each year to push his body and football playing career to new levels of success.

Jerry Rice
Wide Receiver
San Francisco 49ers

Remember:

- The offensive team is made up of eleven players, typically five linemen (two guards, one center, two tackles), two wide receivers, two running backs, one tight end and one quarterback.
- The player lined up at the center of the line is called the center. The center hikes to the quarterback.
- The guards, on either side of the center, guard the quarterback.
- The two players who line up next to the guards are called tackles.
- Linemen (the center, guards, and tackles) are the only players on offense who are not allowed to catch a pass.
- The quarterback throws or hands the ball to another player or keeps the ball and runs himself.
- The tight-end plays at the end of the offensive line and his responsibility alternates between catching passes and blocking for other players.
- Running backs are positioned behind the quarterback. They are often given the ball to run, but they are also eligible to catch passes.
- The wide receivers are stationed off to either side of the line. Their job is to catch passes from the quarterback. •

TIMEOUT

To try and explain the decision making process faced by the coach of the offensive team, let's pretend that you are the Coach of the home team, the Good Guys, and you are playing against your all-time nemesis, the Bad Guys. Let's go through a sample **drive,** a series of consecutive offensive plays.

The Bad Guys have just punted to your Good Guys, and your punt returner calls for a fair catch on your own 20-yard line. The game is scoreless so far.

It's now first down and ten yards to go for another first down, referred to as first and ten. To get a new first down, your team needs to move the ball across your own 30-yard line. You have a total of 80 yards left to go to advance your team into the Bad Guys' end zone for a touchdown.

Since it is only the first down and you know, unless something bad happens like a fumble or interception, that you have three more downs left, you decide to call a pass play. Your quarterback (Passing Pete), takes the snap, takes a few steps back, and throws a perfect **spiral** to your wide receiver (Quick Willy) at your team's 35-yard line. Willy catches the ball and runs for a few more yards before getting tackled on your 40-yard line for a 20 yard gain.

Since your Good Guys advanced the ball for more than ten yards, the next play will be another first and ten situation. So now your team is on its own 40-yard line (with 60 yards to go for a touchdown). To get another first down, you need to get the ball to the 50-yard line, also known as the **midfield** stripe. It's first down again. You are thinking of throwing a pass, but you think the defense may be expecting a pass and decide to play it a little more conservatively. You send in a signal to the quarterback for a running play, so Pete hands the ball off to Rudy the running back, who grabs the ball and runs for three yards before he is tackled.

It is now second down and seven yards to go on your own 43-yard line. Remember, you started with first down at your own 40 and picked up three yards. You decide to try another passing play, but this time to Tony your tight end. Tony is well covered by the defense and drops the ball instead of catching it.

Because the pass was incomplete, the ball is placed back on your 43-yard line. An incomplete pass means the ball goes back to the line of scrimmage from before that play. Now you face third and seven on your 43. You decide to call another pass play to try to pick up the needed yardage. Willy runs 20 yards downfield to the defense's 37-yard line (seven yards to midfield and then another thirteen into the opponent's territory) and catches a pass from Pete. After he catches the ball, Willy runs twelve more yards to the opponent's 25-yard line before he is brought down by the defensive safety, the last line of defense.

You are in good field position now and you've again earned another first down. It's now first and ten on the Bad Guys' 25-yard line. You decide to pass again, but no receiver is able to get open. Unable to find a passing target, Pete is sacked from behind by a defensive lineman. He is tackled behind the line of scrimmage on the opponent's 30 for a loss of five yards.

You now have to cover the original ten yards plus the additional five yards that you just lost to gain another first down. It is second down and fifteen yards to go. Pete throws a short pass to Rudy. Rudy breaks a tackle at the 20-yard line and scrambles all the way downfield to the Bad Guys' five-yard line.

Only five more yards left to go to score a touchdown and you've earned a first down again. On the next play, Pete hands the ball off to Ricky, your other running back, and Ricky finds a hole in the defense and runs across the goal line for the score.

Congratulations, your team has just scored its first touchdown with you as an NFL coach. The Good Guys score six points and have a 6-0 lead.

The Good Guys line up again across from the Bad Guys to try for an extra point. Your team lines up on the two yard line and your kicker, Karl, kicks the ball through the goal posts for an extra point.

The score is now

Good Guys   7
Bad Guys   0.

THE DEFENDERS

The role of the defense...

The **defense** starts the play without possession of the ball and tries to reclaim it. The defensive player's role is to try and prevent the offense from advancing and scoring.

You may hear an attorney in a courtroom use the phrase "the defense rests". Well, in football the defense never rests. The defense is paid to run into people and knock them down. Failure can mean losing the game.

The defense can stop the offense from advancing the ball one of several ways:

- The defense can tackle an offensive player who is carrying the ball. The play is over when a defender causes the ball-carrier's knee or body to touch the ground. If one player transfers the ball to another before being tackled, either by handing it (a **hand-off**) or by throwing it (a **forward pass** or a **lateral**), the defense's target becomes the new player who has the ball.

- The defense can push the offensive player with the ball out of bounds. A player is **out of bounds** if any part of his body touches outside the field of play.

- The defense can knock the football out of the hands of the offensive player, causing a **fumble.** When the ball is dropped by a player who had possession of it, the ball is a **live ball.** This means the play continues and any player can dive on the ball and take possession or pick up the ball and run with it until tackled. If a defensive player has the ball when the play ends, his team now gets to start an offensive series.

- The defense can prevent the offense from completing a forward pass by deflecting the ball or otherwise guarding (**covering**) the receiver. Once the ball has touched the ground on a forward pass, the play is over. An **incomplete** forward pass is not a live ball.

- The defense can catch (or **intercept**) a pass which was intended for an offensive pass receiver. A player making an **interception** can run with the ball until tackled.

Defensive strategies...

The defensive team uses different strategies to counter-act an offensive running play than it does to defend against a passing play. On running plays, defensive players are focused on tackling the offensive player who is carrying the ball, usually a running back.

On passing plays a defensive player may try to tackle the quarterback with the ball before the quarterback can throw a pass. This pursuit is called the **pass rush** and it is called a **sack** if the quarterback is brought down for a loss (behind the line of scrimmage). Once the ball is thrown, a defensive player can try and intercept the ball in midair as the ball is en route to the intended receiver. Alternatively the defensive player can block the receiver from catching the pass, by deflecting the pass or knocking it out of the receiver's hand. A defensive player cannot tackle a receiver before the receiver touches the ball. If a receiver catches the ball, it becomes the responsibility of the defense to tackle him as quickly as possible.

Kansas City Chiefs defensive end Neil Smith and linebacker Jerrol Williams sack Denver Broncos quarterback John Elway in a game in early October, 1994.

Reggie White
Defensive Lineman
Philadelphia Eagles &
Green Bay Packers

FUN FACT

Reggie White, formerly of the Philadelphia Eagles and currently playing for the Green Bay Packers, is one of the most impressive defensive linemen who has ever played the game. With 157 career sacks through the end of the 1995-1996 season, White is the NFL's all-time career sack leader. White has other interests in addition to football—he is also an ordained Baptist minister and is often referred to as the "Minister of Defense".

The three layers of the defense...

The defensive team is made up of **defensive linemen** (in front, opposite the offensive linemen), **linebackers** (in back of the linemen), and the **secondary.** The secondary consists of the **cornerbacks** and **safeties.** The term secondary makes sense if you consider that these players represent a secondary line of defense once an offensive player has gotten past the players responsible for defending the line of scrimmage. Another name for the secondary is the **defensive backfield,** which means the same thing.

A typical defensive formation is shown below. There are many variations, so don't get confused if you see a different configuration. (For extra credit, see explanations of the **4-3** and **3-4 formations** in the glossary.)

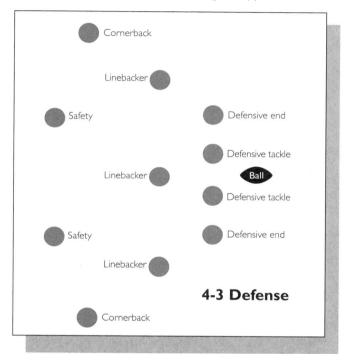

Cornerback

Linebacker

Safety

Defensive end

Defensive tackle

Linebacker

Ball

Defensive tackle

Safety

Defensive end

Linebacker

4-3 Defense

Cornerback

*Alonzo Spellman
Defensive Line*

Defensive linemen...

Defensive linemen are usually very big and powerful like offensive linemen. However, quickness is more important for the defensive linemen than for offensive linemen. Defensive linemen have to be strong so they can get by the equally large offensive linemen, and quick so they can chase down the quarterback once they have made it to the offensive backfield. The defensive linemen want to minimize the amount of time the quarterback has to find an open receiver.

Defensive linemen are called defensive **tackles** and defensive **ends.** It's easy to remember where the ends

*Russell Maryland
Defensive Line
ex-Dallas Cowboy,
now an Oakland Raider*

play—on the end. Tackles line up just inside and right next to the ends. You may remember that there are also offensive players known as ends (tight ends) and tackles. Football wasn't designed to be simple.

William Perry
Defensive Lineman
Chicago Bears

FUN FACT

William "The Refrigerator" Perry played for the Chicago Bears in the late 1980s and early 1990s. Massive in size, Perry fluctuated between 320 and 360 pounds in weight, but he had surprising speed for a player his size. A defensive lineman, Perry was selected twice to the NFC Pro Bowl team. Although "the fridge" was a defensive star, his coach Mike Ditka occasionally used Perry as a running back on offense because he was difficult to tackle. In his most famous moment, Perry ran the ball for a touchdown to help the Bears defeat the New England Patriots 46-10 in Super Bowl XX.

The defensive line pursues the quarterback on a passing play until the quarterback either is **sacked** or throws the ball. A well-timed sack can change the momentum of a game, firing up the defense while deflating the morale of the offense. This is why a player making a sack often celebrates as if he just won the lottery.

Bruce Smith
Defensive End
Buffalo Bills

FUN FACT

Bruce Smith, a perennial pro-bowl selection, plays defensive end for the Buffalo Bills and is a converted fitness fanatic. When he was selected as the number one pick in the 1985 draft, Smith weighed over 300 pounds. He hated to miss a meal and would often gain as much as five pounds in a day. Today, Smith weighs 273 pounds (at 6'4') with his body fat, at times, close to 6%. Smith hates fat on his body and in his diet and has learned to discipline himself to refrain from eating fatty foods, such as red meat and nuts. Smith's fitness activity of choice is a StairMaster™ machine, which he uses in his home even after a day of practice. Smith is known to have broken StairMaster™ machines from intensity and overuse.

Linebackers...

Linebackers, a few yards in back of the linemen, need to be strong to tackle sprinting running backs and quick to help cover receivers or passing plays. Typically, linebackers are smaller than linemen but larger than safeties and cornerbacks. Linebackers are responsible for covering large portions of the field.

Cornerbacks...

Cornerbacks are positioned behind the linebackers and at the back corners on defense. Cornerbacks must be among the fastest players on a team to keep up with speedy offensive receivers. They also help to chase down running backs who have made it past the defensive line and linebackers.

Deion Sanders
Cornerback, Safety as well as
Wide Receiver on offense.
Dallas Cowboys

FUN FACT

Jack "Hacksaw" Reynolds, linebacker for the Los Angeles Rams and the San Francisco 49ers from 1970 to 1984, earned his nickname "Hacksaw" by sawing a 1953 Chevrolet in half. At the University of Tennessee during his senior year, Reynolds' team was badly beaten in an embarrassing defeat that prevented the team from receiving an invitation to the Sugar Bowl (not to be confused with the Super Bowl). The legendary story claims that after the game, he was so angry that he found a beat up, deserted old car, bought a supply of hacksaws and proceeded to rip the car completely apart.

Jack Reynolds
Linebacker
Los Angeles Rams &
San Francisco 49ers

Safeties...

Safeties are often positioned the furthest back of all defensive players, primarily providing defense against the pass. They are essentially the defense's safety net against a long gain by the offense. Like the cornerbacks, the safeties must be very fast. Safeties and cornerbacks are typically the smallest players on the defense, but they must be tough enough to tackle offensive players who are much bigger.

A few defensive strategies...

It's a good idea to be familiar with two main types of defensive strategies for covering the offense. The **man to**

Ronnie Lott
Defensive Back
San Fransico 49ers

man defense is just as it sounds. Each linebacker and defensive back is assigned to cover his own offensive player. In the **zone defense,** each linebacker and defensive back is assigned to cover a particular zone on the field (each is responsible for an area as opposed to a man).

It's also helpful to know the definition of a **blitz,** which is similar to the German warfare term blitzkrieg. A blitz occurs when the defensive linemen are joined by one or more linebackers, cornerbacks or safeties in rushing the quarterback. A blitz exerts extra pressure on the quarterback to pass the ball quickly, so it increases the probability of a sack. Nobody on the offensive line has been pre-assigned to block this surprise rusher, but the offense tries to detect a blitz and to shift blocking assignments. The downside of a blitz is that it may leave an offensive receiver uncovered by a defender.

FUN FACT

Ronnie Lott, who played in the NFL from 1981 to 1995, is considered one of the toughest and most passionate defensive backs to ever play the game. Lott took football so seriously that, after an injury to his finger, he elected to have part of his finger amputated rather than undergo surgery which would have delayed his return to the game. Although brutal on the field, Lott is a dedicated community activist who founded "All Stars Helping Kids", a charity organization dedicated to raising money for disadvantaged children. Read what Ronnie Lott has to say about preparing for games in Chapter Fourteen, The Pre-Season.

Remember:

- Defensive linemen are called defensive tackles and defensive ends.

- Linebackers line up in back of the defensive linemen.

- The secondary consists of the cornerbacks and safeties who line up behind the linebackers.

- A blitzing team sends one or more extra players after the quarterback.

THE "SPECIAL" ONES

I n addition to offensive and defensive squads, a football team also has **special teams** — players who have very specific roles at certain key points in the game. No, these players aren't any more "special" than other players on the team, they just have special assignments and are not on the field as long.

Special teams come on to the field for **kickoffs, field goal** attempts, **extra point** attempts, and **punts.** They are also called **kicking teams** and **receiving teams.** Most special team assignments require quickness and strength. As with all positions in football, players are assigned to roles that match their size, speed, and skills.

FUN FACT

Special teams players are often involved in some of the most exciting plays and jarring collisions on the field. According to Brent Novoselsky (former tight end and special teams player for the Minnesota Vikings) some of the terms that players use, among themselves, to describe these hard hits are:

Snot bubblers
Slobber knockers
Ear hole shots

The Kicking Game...

Football involves three types of kicks and several different situations in which they are used. The types of kicks are the **free kick,** the **place kick** and the punt. Each team typically has one player who does kickoffs and place kicking (kicks held in place by a holder – kicks for extra point attempts and field goal attempts) and another who specializes in punts and free kicks.

Kicking off...

Kickoffs start off the game and the second half. Each team automatically gets to kick off once and receive once. The initial kickoff is decided by a coin toss before the game, with the winning team typically electing to receive the kickoff to start the game. The other team then gets to receive the kickoff to start the second half.

Kickoffs also take place after a team scores a touchdown (following the extra point attempt) or a field goal. The team which just scored kicks off to the opposing team, thereby returning the ball to the team which has just been scored against.

HELPFUL HINT

Sometimes the kicker will attempt to help his team (the kicking team) try to recover the ball on a kickoff. Usually this will happen when the kicking team is trailing and running out of time. An **onside kick** attempt occurs when the kicker tries to kick the football so that it bounces and goes just beyond the required ten yards. This can cause confusion among the receiving team, particularly since some players on the receiving team are selected for their size and blocking ability and not for their ability to catch the ball. The risk to the kicking team of an onside kick attempt is that if the receiving team does recover the ball, the receiving team starts its possession in the kicking team's territory.

FUN FACT

Many players refer to special teams as "suicide squads" because the injury rate is much greater for these players. Imagine the collisions that result from a group of over 200 lb. players lining up on opposite ends of the field and running into each other after picking up speed for 60 yards.

The kickoff originates from the kicking team's 30-yard line. The ball is placed on a plastic holder (a **tee**) and is kicked by the kicking team's place kicker. The kickoff must go at least ten yards downfield (the ball must cross the kicking team's 40-yard line) and stay inside the sidelines, or the kicking team is subject to a penalty. Once the ball has traveled ten yards or is touched by the receiving team, it is a **live** ball (see Chapter Three, The Aggressors), and either

---

FUN FACT

A kick return is measured for the game's statistics by the distance the ball is advanced by the receiving team, beginning at the yard line where the receiving team catches the ball. In rare instances, kick returns can be for over 100 yards. In a game against the Dallas Cowboys on October 21st, 1979, Roy Green of the St. Louis Cardinals returned a kick for over 106 yards. Green caught the ball more than six yards behind his own goal line, eluded a number of would-be tacklers, and ran all the way downfield for a touchdown.

---

team may catch it or pick it up and claim possession. In most cases, the ball is recovered by the receiving team, who runs it back towards the kicking team's goal line until the player who is carrying the ball is tackled. This is often referred to as the **runback** or the **kick return.**

Usually, the kicker will try to kick the ball downfield as far as he can. If the ball goes into the end-zone, then the receiving team has the option of running out of the end zone with it or **downing** the ball for a **touchback.** The kick returner can down the ball by either calling for a **fair catch** (see description which follows under punt) in the end zone or by touching one knee down on the field. A touchback also occurs when the kicker kicks the ball past the receiving team's end zone. In the event of a touchback, the receiving team automatically starts with the ball on its own 20-yard line.

The kicker is often the smallest player on a football team, but once he kicks off he has the same desire as his teammates — to stop the receiving team from advancing the ball towards his goal line. This can lead to funny (and occasionally heroic) scenes when a 140 lb. place kicker attempts to tackle a 220 lb. kick returner.

Field goal...

The offense can attempt a **field goal** on any down, but usually will try on fourth down. If the ball is kicked through (or over) the goal posts, sometimes called the uprights, the offense earns three points.

A field goal attempt rarely occurs on a down other than fourth down, because the team with the ball will usually try for a first down to preserve the option of scoring a touchdown. One rare exception when a coach will call for a field goal attempt on an earlier (first, second, or third) down is when time is running out in the first half or in the game.

On a field goal attempt, the offensive center hikes the ball to a holder who holds it on its end for the field goal kicker, who steps up and kicks it. The ball is customarily held seven yards behind the **line of scrimmage.** Thus if the line of scrimmage is the defense's 20-yard line, the total distance the ball must travel is 37 yards (seven to the line of scrimmage, 20 to the goal line, and ten yards through the end zone to the goal posts). This is known as a 37-yard field goal attempt.

> **HELPFUL HINT**
>
> One trick a place kicker may use is sometimes referred to as a **squibbler** or a **squib kick.** In this case, the kicker kicks the ball downfield but tries to keep it low and bouncing. Because the football is oval-shaped, it can take unpredictable bounces and become difficult to catch once it has hit the ground. A squibbler is sometimes used when the receiving team has a kick returner who is a particularly quick runner and the kicking team is worried about a long runback.

> **HELPFUL HINT**
>
> On a field goal attempt, the kicking team can try for a first down instead by using a passing or running play. This is known as a fake field goal attempt, and the defending team must be prepared for such a play.

Ref signalling field goal is good

If the field goal attempt is unsuccessful, then the opposing team takes possession of the ball from the spot of the attempted kick or the defending team's 20-yard line, whichever is further from the goal line.

FUN FACT

The longest field goal in an NFL game (63 yards), was kicked by Tom Dempsey of the New Orleans Saints against the Detroit Lions on November 8, 1970. Dempsey, who was born with no toes on his right (kicking) foot, has held this record for 26 years.

A field goal may or may not make sense in certain situations. The decision to try a field goal and settle for a maximum of three points instead of "going for it" and trying to score a touchdown or a first down is often one of the toughest decisions a coach must make during a game. The following are some of the factors that weigh into a coach's decision of whether or not to try a field goal:

1. **The distance from the line of scrimmage to the goal line** affects the probability of a successful kick. The closer the offensive team is to the opponent's goal line, the greater the probability of a successful field goal attempt.

2. **The distance needed by the offense to gain a first down or touchdown** also figures heavily. If only a few yards are needed to gain a first down or touchdown, the temptation is greater for the offensive team to "go for it" instead of kicking.

3. **The score of the game** at the time of the decision is another major factor. A team that is very far behind its opponent might not try for a field goal if the three points won't make enough of a difference in the game.

4. **Time remaining** in the game is also key. If it is early in the game, a team might want to play conservatively and get some points on the scoreboard by kicking a field goal. If time is running out, a field goal can be enough to help put the game out of the opponent's reach (for example, extending a lead from

thirteen points to sixteen points in the fourth quarter).

5. The talent on the relevant offensive, defensive, and special teams squads also figures in to the coach's calculation. A team with a star running back may be more inclined to try for a short yardage first down instead of a field goal. The strength and accuracy of the offensive team's place kicker also figures into this equation, particularly for field goal attempts over 40 yards.

Extra Points...

The extra point attempt takes place immediately following a touchdown. The team that has just scored the touchdown has the opportunity of trying for one or two extra points. The extra point (kicking) attempt is like a field goal, but the ball is hiked from the defending team's two yard line. Extra point (kicking) attempts have a high probability of success because of the short distance. The extra point and the two-point play options are described in Chapter One, Training Camp.

Punts...

The **punter** is a player called onto the field, usually on a fourth down play, when the offensive team is not close enough to attempt a field goal and the coach decides not to try for a first down or a touchdown. If the offensive team appears likely to turn the ball over to the defense, the offense's coach wants its opponent to be as far from scoring as possible. The offensive team can elect to **punt** on fourth down, kicking the ball downfield to make it more difficult for the other team to score a touchdown. After a good punt, the ball can be 40 to 50 yards or more further downfield. You can see how this makes it harder for the other team to score, as they have so much further to travel.

As with a kickoff, the receiving team on a punt will typically seek to run the ball back downfield **(kick return)** toward the kicking team's goal line, while the kicking team will attempt to tackle the kick returner. Returning punts is one of the roughest jobs in the game, and it is usually reserved for young, quick players.

> ## HELPFUL HINT
>
> Yard lines are measured between the end zone and midfield. There is no 51-yard line in football, but there is one 50-yard line (midfield), two 49-yard lines, two 48-yard lines, etc. As an example, an offensive receiver who catches a pass on his own 45-yard line and then runs forward for 20 more yards crosses the 50-yard line, then the defense's 45-yard line and 40-yard line, before being brought down on his opponent's 35-yard line.

Jeff Gossett
Punter
Oakland Raiders

In 1994, Eddie Murray of the Dallas Cowboys kicks the game winning field goal to beat the N.Y. Giants.

FUN FACT

Rich Karlis of the Minnesota Vikings, was the only NFL player to kick seven field goals in seven attempts in one game. The game took place on November 5, 1989 when the Vikings beat the Los Angeles Rams 23-21 thanks to Karlis' flawless performance. If Karlis had missed even one of the field goal attempts, the Vikings would have lost the game.

HELPFUL HINT

As with a field goal, the kicking team can fake a punt and try for a first down.

A punt begins when the center hikes the ball to the punter, who catches it, holds it out in front of him, drops it, and kicks it before it falls to the ground. On a punt, there is no player holding the ball for the kicker like on a field goal attempt. Unlike the field goal kicker, the punter works alone in the backfield.

Like on a field goal, the receiving team can attempt to block a punt.

A **fair catch** can be signaled by the player who is going to catch the ball on a punt. The next play will start from the spot where the ball was caught. A player will call for a fair catch if he believes there is limited opportunity to advance the ball because he is likely to get tackled immediately after catching it. When a punt has good hang time,

Jeff Gossett

FUN FACT

Jeff Gossett , the punter for the Oakland Raiders since 1988 and a multi-year AFC Pro Bowl (all-star team) selection, describes the qualifications for being a punter as strong and quick legs (long legs help), flexibility, good athleticism and a competitive nature. Gossett, like may football players, has his own superstitions surrounding a game. He admits that before the game, he avoids using the middle urinal in the bathroom because punters are never supposed to punt the ball down the middle of the field. Gossett fears that if he uses the middle urinal, he will cause himself to punt the ball down the middle.

the kicking team can be descending on or waiting near the kick returner when the ball comes down. The rules make it illegal for the defensive player to tackle or touch the receiver making a fair catch. Since the punt returner is provided with this protection, he gives up the right to run with the ball when he makes a fair catch

Importantly, a fair catch also prevents a player from being flattened by the opposing players running toward him at full speed. Should a receiver attempting to make a fair catch touch the ball without actually catching it (called a **muff**), the ball is live and can be recovered by the opposition but cannot be advanced down the field. In this case, the kicking team goes back on offense.

As on a kickoff, a fair catch signaled in the end zone on a punt reception signifies that the receiving team has elected a **touchback.** The next play starts on the receiving team's 20-yard line. Alternatively, a runner will sometimes catch the ball in the end zone and run it back out in anticipation of advancing it further down the field than the 20-yard line. The possibility of a player catching the ball on a punt and running all the way downfield for a touchdown adds to the game's excitement.

Remember:

- Special teams come onto the field for punts, kickoffs, field-goal attempts and extra point attempts.

- The kickoff originates from the kicking team's 30-yard line at the beginning of each half, after a field goal and following an extra point attempt.

- The offensive team can elect to go for it, punt, or attempt a field goal on a fourth down situation, depending on a number of factors including field position.

- A fair catch of a kick can be made by the receiving team on punts where no advance seems likely.

- A touchback occurs when a player catches the ball (on a kickoff or a punt) in the end zone, and signals a fair catch or downs the ball. A touchback also occurs when the ball is kicked out of (beyond) the end zone.

HELPFUL HINT

A good punter should be able to kick the ball far but also high. A good punt is rated on distance, placement, and time the ball remains in the air. This last element is called **hang time.** The longer the hang time, the more time the kicking team has to get downfield for the tackle. If the punt goes out of bounds, the ball is placed on the yard line where it went out of bounds.

HELPFUL HINT

A player will signal a fair catch on a punt by raising either hand over his head before catching the ball.

TAKING THE FIELD

O.K. learning about the field doesn't sound that exciting, but there are some important points in this chapter that you should learn. So, scan this brief chapter and pay attention to the words in bold.

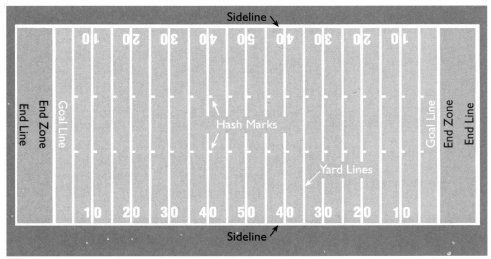

The Boundaries...

The football field is sometimes referred to as the **gridiron.** Football is played on a rectangular field 120 yards long, 100 yards of playing field with a ten yard end zone at each end. The field is 53 1/3 yards wide. When you hear someone say, "it's about as long as a football field," they probably mean 100 yards. The field is marked on all four sides by a

HELPFUL HINT

The field is covered with either **astroturf** (a green synthetic surface, the equivalent of plastic outdoor carpeting) or natural grass. Astroturf is easier to maintain, always looks new, doesn't get muddy in the rain, and doesn't need sunlight or water. The problem with astroturf, though, is that it is not as soft and "forgiving" as natural grass and therefore causes more injuries to players when they hit the ground after a collision. One of the most common astroturf injuries is "turf-toe", an ailment caused when players repeatedly jam their toes inside their shoes due to the superior traction of astroturf. Natural grass is more traditional, but tougher to maintain. Grass is easier on player's bodies but more likely to turn into a muddy swamp in heavy rainfall.

white border called a **boundary line.** The **sideline** refers to the boundary along the side of the field, while the **end line** defines the boundary at the far end of the end zone. A player is considered out of bounds, or outside the field of play, if he steps on or outside these lines.

The end zone...

The **goal line** at each end of the field marks the beginning of the **end zone.** The goal line is ten yards in from, and parallel to, the end lines. The distance between the goal line and the end line is called the end zone (the end zone is usually colored differently, making it easy to distinguish). The essence of football is to move the ball across your opponent's goal line into his end zone and prevent him from moving it into your end zone. When a player makes it into the other team's end zone with possession of the ball, he has scored a touchdown or a two point conversion immediately after a touchdown. You also always want to avoid letting your opponent tackle a member of your team with the ball in your own end zone, resulting in a safety.

Markings on the field...

The field is divided by nineteen white lines marking every five yards, called **yard lines.** These marks help the team know how far it is from the end zone. The 50-yard line is also called midfield. When an announcer states that the offensive team (the team trying to score the touchdown) is at the opponent's 35-yard line, he is describing how far the offense needs to go in the defending team's territory to score a touchdown.

The other group of lines called **hash marks** are also important in determining where a play begins. The two sets of hash marks are located along the center of the field and extend from one end of the field to the other. When a ball goes out of bounds or a play ends between the hash marks and the sidelines, the ball is placed at the closest hash mark for the start of the next play.

The goal posts...

The two y-shaped metal structures jutting out of the ground at the end of both sides of the field are called the **goal posts.** Teams try to kick the ball through the goal posts on field goal attempts and extra point attempts. The goal posts are eighteen feet, six inches apart, and the crossbar is ten feet above the ground. The base of each goal post is padded so players colliding into the bar will not get hurt.

The goal posts were permanently moved to the back of the end zone in 1933 when the Chicago Bears elected, due to a snowstorm, to move their game against the Portsmouth Spartans to an indoor stadium with an 80 yard field. Because the field was so short, the goal posts were moved back from the goal lines to the end lines.

Bronko "Hard Rock" Nagurski

FUN FACT

One would think that football players would notice and try to avoid the goal posts at the end of the end zone because they are painful to run into. A Hall of Famer who played for the Chicago Bears from 1930-1938 and again in 1943, Bronko Nagurski became known as "Hard Rock" when he ran through the defensive line, banged into the goal posts and continued into the brick wall situated behind the end zone. Still a little flustered from the very hard hit, he assumed that he had run into the strongest defensive lineman he had ever encountered.

Working on the chain gang...

Three officials called the **chain crew** or **chain gang** assist the head linesman and are responsible for tracking the number of downs that have been played. They also measure the number of yards that a team needs to go to score a first down. One official holds a sign that keeps track of, and lets the crowd know, what down is being played (first down, second down, etc.). He holds the sign on the sidelines. The other two officials carry two sticks connected by a ten-yard chain. One of the sticks shows where the ball needs to reach for a first down, the **first down marker.** The chain serves as the measuring tool for determining whether a team has gone the required ten yards for a first down. Sometimes the referee will call the chain crew onto the field for a more precise measurement. When the crew makes a measurement, part of the ball must be past the front stick for a first down.

Referee's Signal for a First Down

FUN FACT

Records in the NFL are made to be broken, but Don Shula's record as a head coach of 347 victories is one which can be expected to stand for quite a while and may never be broken. Shula, who retired at the end of the 1995-1996 season, coached for 33 seasons, the first seven with the Baltimore Colts and the last 26 with the Miami Dolphins. In those 33 years, he only had two seasons with more losses than wins. Shula was only 33 years old when he became a head coach in the NFL.

Remember...

- The football field is 100 yards long from goal line to goal line.

- The end zone is ten yards deep and begins at the goal line and ends at the end line.

- The field is divided by yard lines which are marked in five yard increments.

- Goal posts are y-shaped metal structures placed at both ends of the field.

- The chain crew measures whether the ball has been advanced ten yards for a first down. •

John Elway, quarterback of the Denver Broncos, argues with officials for calling his teammate out of bounds.

RULES OF THE GAME

Rules, rules, rules...

Believe it or not, football is a highly structured game, with numerous rules and regulations designed to enforce safe and sportsmanlike play. The rules of football are strictly enforced by the officials. Since the late 1800's, there has been a steady stream of rule changes to make football more exciting, faster-paced, and less dangerous. Unlike baseball, where tradition is considered sacred, in football the rules continue to change from year to year in a continuous effort to improve the game. Don't worry, though. Most of what you read here will still be in the rule book for a while.

Learning every single rule and regulation can be cumbersome, even for the advanced student of football. This chapter will highlight some of the important rules and violations that you'll see and hear about most often. In Chapter Sixteen, you'll learn the referee signals for the commonly called violations. Compare these signals to the action on the field, and before long, you will recognize the penalty which has been called before the television announcer explains it.

Penalties...

A team committing an **infraction** (another word for rule violation) is penalized by moving the ball a specified number of yards towards the goal line of the team being penalized. The more serious infractions are the ones most heavily penalized and therefore awarded the greatest number of yards. Unlike a trial judge who may select from a variety of criminal sentences, the football referee must match the penalty to the infraction according to the rules. The referees signal that a violation has been committed by throwing a yellow handkerchief on the field near the spot where the violation occurred.

FUN FACT:

Football can be a rough game, so players are outfitted with various types of protection. In addition to his helmet (to prevent head and neck injuries), each player wears a mouthpiece to help keep his teeth from getting knocked out. Players wear many different types of pads underneath their uniforms including shoulder pads, hip pads, thigh pads, knee pads, elbow pads and rib pads. All together, a player can sport an extra 50 to 60 pounds of equipment.

An important point to remember about penalties is that the team that did not commit the violation has the option of accepting or rejecting the penalty. Most penalties invalidate the outcome (gain or loss of yardage) on the play when the penalty occurs. If a team accepts a penalty, then the penalty is enforced. If, however, the penalty is declined then the previous play stands as is. A team might choose to reject the penalty if the play that just occurred made its situation better off. For example, if the offensive team scores a touchdown and a penalty is called against the defensive team on that play, the offensive team will reject the penalty so it can keep the touchdown.

Not all infractions are limited to a loss of yardage. Some penalties against the offense include a loss of a down. Other penalties against the defense result in an automatic first down for the offense. And, if a penalty is particularly flagrant or dangerous, a player can be ejected from the game. Thankfully, this ultimate penalty rarely happens in football.

Here's a list of common rules violations. Don't worry about remembering how many yards the penalty is worth or whether there is a loss of down. That will come to you when you watch some games. Just try and remember what each violation means.

Offsides...

There are two commonly called penalties that arise from movement before the ball is hiked:

Defensive offsides occurs when a defensive player's body moves over the line of scrimmage before the ball is snapped. The defense is allowed to move before the ball is hiked, but it cannot move over the line of scrimmage until after the snap.

Referee signalling an offsides penalty

TIME OUT

Here's an example to show how penalties work.

Let's say that your team (the Good Guys) has the ball on offense on your own 30-yard line. On the first play of the series your team gains only two yards. It is now second down and eight yards to go on your own 32-yard line. Your Good Guys have three plays left to move the ball eight more yards to your 40-yard line. On the second down play, your running back (remember Rudy?) gains four yards on a run up the middle. It looks like you face third down and four to go. However, there is a yellow flag on the field. The referee signals that one of the players on defense (as usual, your fierce conference rival, the Bad Guys) has intentionally tripped one of your offensive players who did not have the football at the time. In this situation, the Bad Guys committed the infraction, therefore they will be penalized.

A tripping penalty is worth ten yards, meaning that the team that committed the penalty has the ball moved ten yards closer to its goal line. Since the Bad Guys are playing defense, this means that the offense gets to move the ball ten yards closer to its destination (the end zone). The referee marches off the ten yards from the line of scrimmage towards the defensive

goal line and places the ball on the Good Guys' 42-yard line. The penalty is typically marked from the point where the play started. Since your Good Guys needed to get to the 40-yard line and have made it to the 42-yard line, you have gotten a first down as a result of the penalty. It's first and ten on your own 42.

On the next play, a defensive lineman moves across the line of scrimmage a moment before the ball is snapped. The play continues, and your quarterback Passing Pete completes a pass to Tony the tight end for a ten yard gain. A penalty flag has been thrown, and your team now has the option of accepting or rejecting the penalty. Offsides is a five-yard penalty. If you accept the penalty, you will move the ball five yards from the starting point, to your 47-yard line. If you reject the penalty then your gain on the play counts and you have the ball across midfield on your opponent's 48-yard line. You reject the penalty.

Offensive offsides occurs when an offensive player lines up with any body part past the offensive line of scrimmage (some leeway is given to the center, who has to hike the ball). Once the offensive team goes into its crouching stance (its **set**), the line is not allowed to move at all until the ball is hiked. If the offensive line moves before the snap, this is called a **false start,** whether or not the moving player crosses the line of scrimmage.

Holding...

There are also two versions of holding, offensive and defensive:

Offensive holding occurs when an offensive player, typically a lineman seeking to protect his quarterback, uses his hands to grab the body or clothing of a defensive player. Offensive players are allowed to use their hands and arms to push or block a defensive player, but cannot hold onto him. Sometimes an offensive linemen holds onto his opponent because he thinks no referee can see him, and sometimes he gets away with it. The rules are intended to discourage this type of play.

Defensive holding is not allowed either. A defensive player is not allowed to hold onto an offensive player unless that player has the ball. Defensive holding typically takes place in the defensive backfield, where a defender is tempted to hold on to a pass receiver running a **pattern** in order to slow him down.

Referee signalling a holding penalty

Pass interference...

Another form of penalty which can be called against the defense or the offense is **pass interference:**

Defensive pass interference is the more commonly called of the two. Once a pass has been thrown towards a receiver, the defender is not allowed to interfere, by touching the receiver, with the receiver attempting to catch the ball. (The defender is free to deflect or intercept the ball.) Without this rule, we would see few completed passes in football, since the defender could tackle the receiver before he is able to make a catch.

Offensive pass interference occurs less frequently but is an equally serious infraction. The receiver cannot touch the defender when the ball has been thrown. Without this rule, you would see a lot more receivers pushing the defenders aside to catch the ball.

When a receiver and a defender touch each other unintentionally while each trying to make a play for the ball, there is generally no penalty called. This is known as **incidental contact.**

Offensive penalties...

Some penalties can only be called against the offense:

Intentional grounding occurs in certain situations where the quarterback is behind the line of scrimmage and is about to get sacked. Remember that after an incomplete pass, the next play starts from the prior play's line of scrimmage. If, to avoid a loss of yardage from a sack, the quarterback throws the ball into the ground or to a place where there is no eligible receiver, he can be called for intentional grounding of the football.

An **illegal forward pass** most often occurs when a player (typically the quarterback) runs over the line of scrimmage and then throws a forward pass to a receiver. An offensive player is only allowed to throw a forward pass from behind the original line of scrimmage.

Another form of illegal forward pass occurs when the offense throws more than one forward pass on a given play. This restriction does not apply to passes which go backwards or sideways, called **laterals.** Laterals are not considered forward passes, and there is no limit to how many laterals the offense can use on a play, although more than one on a play is rare.

Remember that a forward pass can only be thrown to an eligible receiver, which excludes linemen from catching a forward pass.

Personal fouls...

Most violations are committed unintentionally or are relatively harmless. There are a few infractions, however, that appear intentional or are unusually unsportsmanlike or dangerous. These violations are called **personal fouls** and carry some of the most severe penalties.

Unnecessary roughness is a personal foul against a player who uses a level of rough play which goes beyond what is necessary to make a block or a tackle. Unnecessary roughness can include kicking or tripping the runner, tackling a player who clearly does not have the ball or is out of bounds, tackling or blocking after the play has

Referee signalling a personal foul penalty

clearly ended, a **(late hit)** or using one's helmet to hurt the opponent (sometimes called **spearing**).

John Elway

FUN FACT

John Elway, the quarterback for the Denver Broncos, was playing his last college game at Stanford University against Stanford's long time rival, the University of California at Berkeley (Cal). The game was important for Stanford because if they won the game, they would be selected to the Peach Bowl (in college football, being chosen to play in a Bowl game is a reward for a successful season of play). John Elway had just masterminded a beautiful last minute drive, leading Stanford down the field to kick a field goal that gave Stanford a 20-19 lead with four seconds left to play in the game.

The kickoff should have been a relative formality, but on the ensuing kickoff, the Cal players used a trick play to keep their hopes alive. Cal players lateralled (passed the ball backwards or sideways) the ball four times among themselves to avoid being tackled with the ball. Thinking, as did most observers in the stands, that the play was over, the Stanford band marched on to the field to celebrate a victory. In the ensuing commotion, the Cal players ran the ball through the Stanford band and into Stanford's end zone for a game winning touchdown.

Clipping is a personal foul which occurs when a player blocks another player from behind or below the waist. Clipping is a serious penalty, because it involves a high risk of injury to the back or knees of the player being **clipped.**

Roughing the passer, another personal foul, occurs when a defender tackles or runs into the quarterback after the **quarterback** has already handed off or passed the ball away, unless the hit is unintentional. While the goal of a defensive lineman is to sack the quarterback, the quarterback is off limits after the ball has left his hand, as he is not expecting to be hit. The NFL goes to great lengths to protect its quarterbacks, its prized assets, from unnecessary injury.

A **face mask** foul arises when a player grabs the face mask of an opposing player's helmet during a play. In making a tackle, players are allowed to grab any part of an opponent from the shoulders down. However, grabbing

Referee signalling a face mask penalty

the face mask risks serious injury to the opponent's neck and is forbidden, whether intentional or not. Face mask violations can be called on either defensive or offensive players. An intentional face mask violation is considered more serious and carries a more severe penalty.

The game clock...

A number of important rules of football do not directly involve penalties but are integral to the game. Many involve the game clock, which runs down continuously with certain exceptions. The clock stops after an incomplete pass or after a player with the ball steps out of bounds. It also stops at the end of a quarter, for a time-out and for the two minute warning. Managing the game clock is an important element of football strategy. For example, a team which is behind late in a game will often throw passes near the sideline in order for the receiver to stop the clock by stepping out of bounds.

Each team is allotted three **time outs** per half. A time out stops the clock for one minute and 50 seconds (40 seconds when there is only two minutes or less left to play in the first or second half) and allows the team who called the time out to reformulate a plan of action. Coaches and players are very careful not to use up a team's time outs early in the game. The team might need to regroup at the end of the game or stop the clock before it runs out.

The **two minute warning** is an automatic time out which occurs when there are only two minutes left in the first half or in the game. The two minute warning is not charged to (it does not use up a time out of) either team. The referee blows the whistle and calls a time out. Often the two minute warning is helpful to a team which is behind in points and needs the extra time to strategize.

Referee signalling a time out

The offense only has 40 seconds after each play, starting when the referee blows his whistle, to begin the next play. A **delay of game** occurs if the offense violates this rule and takes longer than 40 seconds. Without a time limit, the players could stay in the huddle all day and strategize about the next play. (Even the most dedicated fan in the world would have a problem spending twelve hours watching the same football game.) Or, the team with a lead could allow time on the clock to run out without starting another play. •

NFL MEMORABLE MOMENTS

The history of Football is rich with true stories of amazing plays and memorable games. One of the elements making football so exciting to watch is that you never know when you will see a game that makes football history or a play on which a new NFL record is set. Some stories become so famous that they are immortalized with phrases which bring to mind the excitement of the moment. You can't be expected to memorize general trivia such as the name of the player who returned two fumbles for touchdowns in one game, but you can know about the Heidi Game or the Immaculate Reception. (The fumble recoveries were by Fred "Dippy" Evans in case you were wondering.)

The Heidi Game (Oakland Raiders vs. New York Jets in Oakland, 1968)

Viewers were glued to their television sets near the end of a nail-biter of a game which found the Jets beating the Raiders 32-29 with just 61 seconds remaining in the game. The Raiders had possession of the ball on their own 22-yard line and were attempting to beat the clock (and the odds) to try and score. Fans were shocked, however, when an NBC production mix-up abruptly ended the

broadcast of the game to cut to a previously scheduled showing of the movie Heidi, starring Shirley Temple. As football fans cursed the televised image of Shirley Temple unaware of the ending of the game, the Raiders threw for a 43-yard touchdown pass with 50 seconds left to take the lead. On the ensuing kickoff, the Jets fumbled the ball and the Raiders picked it up and ran into the end zone to win the game 43-32. Not known for their shyness, some New York fans were so irate that they called 911 to complain and find out the outcome of the game.

The Immaculate Reception (Pittsburgh Steelers vs. Oakland Raiders, 1972)

The Steelers led the Raiders 6-0 in a divisional playoff game which would end the season for the loser. In the fourth quarter, the scoreless Raiders brought in replacement quarterback Ken Stabler who drove his team 80 yards down the field for a touchdown with 1:13 on the clock to take a 7-6 lead. It looked as if the Raiders had won the game. With just 22 seconds left, Steelers quarterback Terry Bradshaw, trying to salvage a victory, threw a desperation pass to his receiver Frenchy Fuqua. Fuqua was heavily guarded, and the ball bounced off him (or his defender) and appeared to fall to the ground. Before it hit the ground, however, Pittsburgh running back Franco Harris snatched the ball off of the top of his shoes (yes, his shoes). Harris broke a tackle to run the ball into the end zone for a game winning touchdown with just five seconds left.

The Stupor Bowl (also the Stumble Bowl) (Baltimore Colts vs. Dallas Cowboys, 1971)

The Colts and the Cowboys were playing in Super Bowl V, the first Super Bowl championship since the merger of the AFL and NFL. Everyone was anticipating a great game to officially celebrate the merger. However, this game would go down in football history as one of the worst games ever played. There were six fumbles, six interceptions and one blocked field goal attempt. It was amazing that anyone actually won the game, but Baltimore held on to defeat Dallas by a score of 16-13.

The Drive
(Denver Broncos vs.
Cleveland Browns in the
1986 AFC Championship game)

John Elway, the quarterback for the Broncos since 1983, is known as the type of player you would want on your team in the last two minutes of a tight game. Elway has, on many occasions, led his team to stunning victories in the last few minutes of games. One of Elway's most dramatic performances as a pro came to be known as "the Drive" when the Broncos, behind 20-13, had the ball on their own two yard line with 98 yards to go to score a touchdown and time running out on the clock. Few observers would have given the Broncos a chance to come back, given their field position. But Elway led the Broncos downfield to pick up a touchdown and an extra point to tie the game. In overtime, Rich Karlis, (then the kicker for the Broncos) kicked a 33-yard field goal to win the game for the Broncos and send them to the Super Bowl.

John Elway

Garo's Pass
(Miami Dolphins vs.
Washington Redskins, 1973)

The Dolphins were trying to complete the first perfect season in the history of the NFL. They had maintained a perfect record in the regular season, winning fourteen games without a loss. Two more playoff victories brought them to Super Bowl VII, where they looked to make football history against the Redskins. The Dolphins dominated the game and led 14-0 in the fourth quarter when Miami kicker Garo Yepremian (a soccer player from Cyprus) attempted a 42-yard field goal. The kick was blocked by the defense and, to his surprise, bounced right back into Yepremian's arms. Wanting to try and salvage the play, Yepremian saw a teammate downfield and decided to improvise with his first forward pass as an NFL player. The ball slipped out of his hand and went almost straight up in the air, landing in the arms of Redskins cornerback Mike Bass who ran 49 yards for a touchdown which, with the extra point, put the Redskins back in the game. Miami now led 14-7 with 2:07 remaining. Miami, fortunately for Yepremian, held on to win the game and complete their perfect season, a feat which has never been matched in the NFL.

The Sneakers Game (Chicago Bears vs. New York Giants, 1934)

It was a frigid December day in Chicago, and the two teams were playing on a frozen Polo Grounds field. Both teams were finding the playing conditions particularly difficult, because their cleats were unable to grip the hardened field. At halftime, the Giants, behind by a score of 10-3, decided to try switching shoes to see if that would make a difference. When the third quarter began, the Giants walked on the field in sneakers, to the surprise of the Bears. The sneakers made the difference, and the Giants scored 27 more points to win the game 30-13. Today football teams have a variety of footwear available to suit different playing fields and weather conditions.

The Catch (Dallas Cowboys vs. San Francisco 49ers in the 1981 NFC playoff game)

The Cowboys (known as "America's Team") were highly confident going into the NFC playoff game against the 49ers. The 49ers had never been to a Super Bowl and were not considered a real threat to the Cowboys. With four minutes and 54 seconds left in the game, the 49ers were behind 27- 21. San Francisco had the ball on its own eleven yard line, needing an 89-yard drive to score a touchdown. Down by six points at this late point in the game, the 49ers needed more than a field goal to win.

Dwight Clark making "The Catch"

Joe Montana, later to become known as one of the NFL's great quarterbacks, was only 25 years old. With confidence and determination, Montana marched his team down the field to Dallas' six yard line. There were 58 seconds left in the game and the 49ers were facing a third down and three yards to go. The Cowboys defensive linemen, expecting a pass, burst off of the line of scrimmage to go after Montana, and as the play began the young quarterback appeared to be in trouble. Dodging the Cowboys' oncoming defensive linemen, Montana looked downfield and spotted one of his favorite targets, wide receiver Dwight Clark. Clark was surrounded by Dallas players, but nevertheless Montana threw the ball in Clark's direction, very high and close to the sidelines. To the amazement of the players and fans, Clark jumped up above the defenders and came down with the ball for a game winning touch-down. The 49ers went on to win Super Bowl XVI, the first of the team's five Super Bowl championships.

The Career Ending Coin Toss (Washington Redskins vs. New York Giants, 1940)

Normally, the coin toss is a mere formality of the game …what could possibly go wrong? Yet, hall of fame tackle Turk Edwards, playing for the Washington Redskins in 1940, stepped away from a coin toss, turned his knee and had to be carried off the field, thus ending his celebrated football career forever.

The Super Bowl Shuffle (Chicago Bears vs. New England Patriots, 1985-1986)

The 1985 Chicago Bears were so certain of their prospects for Super Bowl XX in New Orleans that they found the time to record a rap video, the Super Bowl Shuffle, before the season was over. In fact, the Bears finished the regular season 15-1 and crushed the New England Patriots 46-10 in the Super Bowl. This team will long be remembered by its famous lyrics: "We're not here to start no trouble. We're just here to do the Super Bowl Shuffle."

William "Refrigerator" Perry

Staubach's Hail Mary (Dallas Cowboys vs. Minnesota Vikings, 1975 NFC Divisional Playoff Game)

Roger Staubach, star quarterback for the Cowboys, was running out of options. His team was losing to the Vikings by a score of 14-10 and, with the ball at midfield, he had only 32 seconds left to try and salvage the game by scoring a touchdown. Rearing back, he threw the ball well downfield into a crowd, hoping that intended receiver Drew Pearson would somehow catch the pass. Pearson eluded his defenders to make the catch, scoring a touchdown for a 17-14 Dallas win. The pass was called a Hail Mary because, as Staubach admitted, he threw the pass up in the air and prayed that someone on his team would catch it. The term Hail Mary is now used by many watchers of the game to describe long passes in desperate situations when the passing team doesn't have much to lose.

Bart Starr shown here with coach Vince Lombardi

The Ice Bowl (Green Bay Packers vs. Dallas Cowboys, 1967)

The Packers were facing the Cowboys in the NFC Championship game on a miserably cold December day when the temperature was thirteen degrees and the wind chill was minus 50. Green Bay was behind by a score of 17-14, with sixteen seconds left to play. Packers quarterback Bart Starr called a play (known as a quarterback sneak) which required him to carry the ball himself across the line of scrimmage and into the end zone. The play worked, as Starr followed a key block from offensive lineman Jerry Kramer to cross the goal line. Green Bay won the game by a score of 21-17.

The Premature Celebration (Dallas Cowboys vs. Buffalo Bills, 1993)

Very little went right for the Buffalo Bills in Super Bowl XXVII. The Bills were losing by an embarrassing 52-17 margin, when Dallas defensive player Leon Lett recovered a Buffalo fumble on his own 35-yard line and ran down the field with it. As Lett approached the Buffalo end zone, he began to celebrate his score a bit too early. As Lett slowed down and began to wave the ball, Bills wide receiver Don Beebe chased him down and stripped the ball out of the hands of the puzzled Cowboy, reclaiming a bit of pride and a Buffalo possession of the ball while earning Lett a place in Super Bowl lore. •

A WEEK IN THE LIFE OF A PROFESSIONAL PLAYER

This section is taken from an extensive interview conducted with Brent Novoselsky, former tight end and special teams player who played pro football from 1988 to 1994. Novoselsky played a season with the Chicago Bears and then played six years with the Minnesota Vikings. Novoselsky ranks third on the Vikings' list for consecutive games played by a tight end. He also made over 100 special team tackles in his career. Novoselsky, who graduated from the University of Pennsylvania's Wharton School of Business, is now an insurance agent with the Greater Chicago Group, and is a wonderfully nice guy. He and his wife Andrea reside in a suburb of Chicago with their two boys Alec and Zachary. He shares, for this book, the ups and downs of a typical week for a pro football player — beginning with the morning after a Sunday game.

Monday morning...

Monday morning was the most sore you've ever felt in your entire life. Monday morning you'd just try to get out of bed, although you wouldn't really get out of bed, you'd just throw your legs over the bed and hope your feet would catch you because everything congealed overnight and was sore. You'd feel worse than you've ever felt in your entire life. All you'd be thinking is that there is no way you would be ready to play by next Sunday. But, you'd know that you would have to be ready.

From 7:00 a.m. to 12:00 noon each player had a specific time when he had to be at practice to start lifting weights. The rookies had to be at practice at 7:00 a.m. I was pretty lucky that I didn't have to go in until 11:00 a.m., which was perfect…it allowed me to sleep in a bit. You really can't sleep on Sunday nights because you're so pumped up from the game you just played, so worried about watching the game film the next day, and so sore. Monday is the hardest lift of the week because you are so sore. You just try to get through it.

Monday afternoon...

At about 2:00, you'd go to meetings and anyone who played special teams would go over special teams films. You may think that you did really well in a game and then see the game on film and say, "I guess I really didn't do that well." Or you may think, "I really screwed up, they're going to cut me" and you look at the film and think, "Oh it's really not that bad." That's the thing about football, you just can't see everything on the field. You might think you helped tackle a guy, but you barely slowed him down. Films are rude awakenings and everyone is just waiting to get chewed out because everyone screws up at least once or twice a game. You're cringing all during the films. It's probably the hardest part of being a professional athlete.

Films usually lasted about half an hour and then at about 2:30 you'd have a team meeting where the head coach would come in and give you a rah, rah speech, tell you where the team was in the season, congratulate you on a good game, or tell you that you needed to play better. Monday provided closure to the week. After the head coach came in, you'd break up offensively and defensively and go over films. Regardless of who was in the game and who was in the particular play on film, you'd pay attention to what they were doing. If that person on film got hurt, you could be playing his position, so you'd better be ready.

When we watched films, we watched from two angles. Coaches used the VCR's to go back and forth over approximately 90 plays, watched from two angles. That's about 180 plays that you'd watch four to five times each, unless you screwed up and then you'd watch them even more. Even though coaches realized it was easy for them to sit back and be armchair quarterbacks (while they were watching films with a cup of coffee), the coaches had to be tough and criticize because their jobs were tied to you. They needed to get on your back and pester you to do the right thing.

About 4:30 or 5:00 Monday, we finished watching films—usually you would watch films in your sweats. A professional football player spends about ten minutes a day in street clothes and the rest of the time in the team's clothes. (After all, you want to sweat in their clothes not yours.) We would put our helmets on (we always practiced with helmets for safety reasons) and we'd go out to the field and do what's called a quick run around–full stretch, jog around, quick run through a few plays–then we were free to go.

Monday night was free...
Tuesday was all yours...

They didn't require it, but they did ask you to get involved in the community. When I was in Minnesota for six years, my wife, Andrea, was in charge of coordinating visits to the local childrens' hospitals. We'd go visit the kids for a couple of hours. Most players would try to get involved somehow. It was your only day off, though, so you really wanted to spend it with your family…that one day was essentially your weekend. You wanted to relax, play with your kids, lie on the couch and just take it easy.

Tuesday night...

You'd try to get to bed at a decent hour because Wednesday was the start of the week. Wednesday, for a football player, is like Monday for an office worker.

Wednesday morning...

During the season, Wednesday or Thursday was your lifting day, depending on your position and your seniority. The rookies had to go in early about 6:00 a.m. and lift, the veterans had it a little easier, about 7:00 or 7:30 a.m. I always had Thursday at 7:30 a.m., so on Wednesday, I didn't have to be at practice until 8:30 a.m. for a special teams meeting. We would go over films, preview the next opponent's personnel and their team films and discuss the game plan for the week.

9:00 Wednesday was a team meeting. The head coach would come in and take care of administrative details and discuss how important this game was to us – his speech changed a bit, depending on what time of the year it was and how many games we had left.

Five minutes after the speech, the rookies would have to get up and close the doors to separate the

Brent Novoselsky surges forward for extra yardage after making a reception.

offense from the defense. In the offensive meetings, the first fifteen minutes were spent taking a look at scouting reports and personnel. The coaches would come up and discuss the next opponent's personnel-who they've got, what they will play, who's hurt, any tendencies, etc.

Then, the offensive coordinator would get up and go through the game plan. We each had a game plan–notebooks with everything you ever wanted to know. They were very extensive…with all the offensive plays drawn up and all of the possible defensive strategies laid out. The offensive coordinator would tell us a little about the other team and we would proceed to go over every single play that could come up. It usually would take an hour and a half to two hours. If you had time you'd break up with your position coach and talk about any special changes related to your position.

Every special teams player always had a back up position on offense or defense and you were always going to extra meetings and practicing all aspects of the game.

From 11:15 to 12:00, we would walk through our plays. The offense would run fifteen plays for the defense and then they would run about fifteen plays for us. They'd try to act like the other team we were about to play, and we would do the same for them.

The walk-through was at a jogging pace and was not full contact. You didn't wear pads or helmets, just sweats.

Wednesday afternoon...

You ate lunch with the team in the cafeteria at noon on Wednesdays and Thursdays. At 1:15 p.m. you would have individual meetings with your position coach and watch more films for 45 minutes.

Special teams practice would start at 2:00 in full dress (uniforms, pads, and helmets). From 2:00 to 2:30 we would focus on special teams items and then at 2:30 the whole team would get together for a fifteen minute stretch and go through the on-field practice which would include:

- Warm-up exercises
- Drills (ten minutes)
- Getting together as a team and walking through some plays
- Some catching drills and catching drills against defensive backs

In the middle of practice (kind of like a half-time break) we would meet for another special teams practice. We would then regroup as a team and go through a passing and running game (seven on seven passing drills-no linemen). Again, we'd bring everyone together and have full contact drills.

At 5:15 p.m. practice was over. The coach would tell you how bad practice was and how you'd have to improve for tomorrow. Some of us would stay after to work on techniques and catching the ball so usually we weren't out of there until 5:45 or so, then a shower and back home.

Thursday–basically the same as Wednesday...

In general, we would not take many breaks during practice, although, as the season progressed we would play NFC Central teams twice, so by the second time we'd find that there was not as much to learn. Most teams tried to beat you physically instead of trying to fool you. The ones that would try and fool you were usually the ones that were struggling and not very good, so we'd end up spending more time looking over their stuff.

Friday...

We would all come in at 8:30 a.m. for a team meeting. Instead of a walk-through at 11:15, we would just start practice.

For Friday's practice, we just needed to wear helmets, which is good because Friday we would do what was called short yardage and goal line, (a drill that simulates an offensive play). That usually lasted from 11:15 to 1:30, and then we had lunch. We usually got together as a team for lunch and had one of the positions on the team buy for everyone. We would switch off the position each week.

Friday night was free...

Saturday...

At 9:00 am. you would meet to go over films of the previous day's practice. (Every day you would go through films of previous practices and correct the things you did wrong.)

Saturday's practice was pretty light. We would wear shorts and no pads, but we'd wear helmets.

If we had an out of town game, we usually tried to leave so we could get in around dinner time. (The coach didn't like us to get in too early and have too much time on our hands.)

So, we usually got in around 5:00 or 5:30 p.m. Each player would get a per diem meal allowance of $33, which for hungry football players just about paid for the appetizers. After dinner, we would get back to the hotel and get ready for a special teams meeting at 9:00 p.m. At 9:30 p.m. we would have offensive and defensive meetings, then at 10:00, the whole team would get together for a meeting. At 10:05, we would have a team snack and then go back to our rooms for curfew at 11:00p.m.

If we were playing at home, it was basically the same routine. We'd have practice Saturday morning and then we would check in to the local hotel between 6:00 and 8:00 p.m. We still would have our 9:00 p.m. meeting. We would try and keep things consistent even at home. It gets you into a familiar position, familiar with your surroundings. You've done this for so many years you have a certain pre-game mind set that gets you mentally ready.

Everyone had a ritual before a game. It usually started on Saturday nights. My routine was basically the same. I would eat the same things every Saturday night, wear the same t-shirts, sit in the same place on the bench, stretch in the same place...anything that was consistent. The night before I would always eat a Caesar salad and pasta. Then I would eat ice-cream and have cookies and milk while watching Saturday Night Live.

Sunday morning (game day)...

We were all required to be at the stadium two hours before game time, which is an NFL rule. Buses would leave from the hotel in time to get us there. At home games we would drive ourselves to the stadium.

For 12:00 games, we would get there by 10:00 a.m. except for the offensive linemen...

Most of the offensive linemen would get to the stadium at 7:00 a.m., dress in full uniform, sit down surrounding a cooler of Mountain Dew, and drink soda for four hours until the rest of the team arrived.

Offensive linemen are a special breed – they'd do everything together. They're so close and such a cohesive unit. The offensive line is unique.

At 10:00 we would get our pants on, go on the field, look around, look up in the stands to try and prepare ourselves mentally for the game. It was kind of an eerie feeling looking at the stands before the fans got there. It was good for us to familiarize ourselves with the stadium because we wouldn't want to be looking around as we were about to start the game on kickoff.

It was a little bit of a home-field advantage when you're home. You knew the fans and were comfortable at the stadium. My favorite stadium (other than home field) was Soldier Field. I grew up there and knowing that I can stand on the field, look up and see the skyscrapers has always been a real thrill for me. It's also nice playing on natural grass.

Game time...

45 minutes before game time we'd go through a mini practice to get loose. We would head back in the locker room fifteen minutes before the game for a team prayer and last speech from the head coach. He'd say something like, "we need this game, got to beat the Packers because they're in our division."

About five minutes before the game started, we would walk out together as a team to get introduced to the fans. We would slap hands and generally get pumped. The captains would go out for the coin toss to start the game. The captains were usually chosen for their leadership abilities. Some teams, like the Vikings, changed captains every week and some teams kept the same captain all year. I was fortunate enough to be chosen captain eighteen times in my six years with the Vikings.

When I was the captain and I made the call for the coin flip, it added another dimension to my nervousness about the game. It was tough because you'd have this controlled response for aggression. Every time I hear the star spangled banner, I want to hit something because I get so pumped up–it's a mindset. And you have to be ready.

You're always nervous before the first play — no two ways about it — no matter what you're doing. You're thinking, can I do this? Can I block this guy? Can I run down and make the tackles? After the first play, you realized it would be o.k., and you would not really be nervous the rest of the game, but you would get upset – and you would get excited. It was a long process so you'd try and stay on an even keel. You were definitely going to get tired.

The first two quarters were intense, then came halftime.

Halftime–try to recharge...

Since they cut halftime down to twelve minutes from fifteen minutes, the most important thing you would have to do at halftime is go to the bathroom. You'd been drinking a lot of water and Gatorade during the game and so this was mostly what you'd think of. There wasn't much time for anything else.

The Coach would come in for a few minutes and say something short–no time for long drawn out speeches. Halftime was really meant to be the time for the offensive/defensive coordinators to take over and say what we had to do in the second half to win. It was a time to retool our strategy. Usually the offense and defense were broken up. Depending on what stadium we played in, we might go off in different rooms to strategize, but again, there wasn't that much time.

Brent Novoselsky catching a pass for a Viking touchdown.

The second half...

The second half had a familiar feel. You knew the guys better and you knew what needed to be done in order to win. Most teams feel that they beat themselves. It's really like the last stretch of a marathon—who's got the kick left.

The fourth quarter...

It's do or die—nothing to save. "Just leave it all out on the field" as they say. You wanted to be exhausted when the game was over. Winning teams find some way to pull it out and losing teams find some way to lose. It's all about a winning attitude. Some teams have it and some teams don't. The league is pretty equal, it's just that some teams know how to win. It's kind of an intangible thing—not necessarily physical. Winning teams seem to have an aura about them.

Game over...

We'd shake hands with the other team and say a few words to the players on the opposing team that we knew. We'd then go over to the sideline, say hi to our wives, and take pictures with our sons or daughters while still in uniform. We would then go back to the locker room for a team prayer and to collect our thoughts.

We would also hear a short speech from the head coach, whether we won or lost, about not playing well enough and what we should have done better. The speeches were still pretty upbeat, though, because the coach knew we had more games to play in the season and he didn't want to get us down.

Most of us would stay after the game for ice, taping and showers. Then we would head over to the players' lounge where we met our families. If it was a home game, we would try and get together with some of the other players' families. We'd usually go grab some dinner with them.

If it was a 12:00 game, we'd usually be out by 4:00. If it was a night game, we didn't get together with the other families afterward because it was too late. When you got home, you would climb into bed and all you could think about was how sore you were going to be when you woke up the next morning for the Monday morning lifting session. The excitement of playing next Sunday's game, however, made it all worthwhile. •

10

THE HISTORY OF THE NFL

From its inception in the late 1880's, football has continually evolved and transformed. Football grew out of the sports of soccer and rugby, adopting many of their rules and practices while inventing many of its own unique characteristics. This section tells you how football evolved into what it is today. Learning about the history of the game may give you some further insight into its rules and traditions.

In the beginning...

In the 1800's, soccer was the sport of the century until a group of college students decided that they wanted to make the sport more exciting by adding the option of carrying the ball in addition to the soccer style of just kicking the ball.

In 1869 a game (very much resembling soccer) was played between Rutgers and Princeton. Even though this match largely resembled a soccer game, it did incorporate some football elements, like catching the ball and blocking. Many historians claim that this was the first football game, however some insist that this game was too much like soccer to be characterized as a genuine football match. Whichever side you take on this debate, it is clear that football was slowly evolving.

McGill University (of Montreal, Canada) challenged Harvard University in 1874 to this soccer-like game of football. McGill and Harvard each had different ideas about the rules of the game. Harvard was playing more of a kicking game while McGill was playing more of a passing and running game like

The introduction of the forward pass helped change the game of football.

Bronko Nagursky starred for the Chicago Bears in the 1930's.

rugby. The two schools could not agree on which game to play so they decided to play two games. One would be the soccer-like game and the other would be the rugby-like game. After playing both versions, Harvard whole-heartedly embraced the rugby version and soon other colleges followed suit. This rugby-like game was still very far from the football we know today, but the sport was developing.

In 1876, Harvard and Yale, formed the Intercollegiate Football Association (IFA) and began instituting many of the significant changes that led to a more organized and structured game. Walter Camp, known as the father of football, was a running back from Yale who envisioned the game as a mental and physical exercise requiring planning, strategy, and order. In the following years, Camp changed the rules that made rugby into football.

A dangerous game...

As football continued to evolve and gain recognition, the injury rate skyrocketed. If you think football is rough now, you should have seen it then. Players did not wear any special protection and there were no penalties called for excessively rough play. One particularly dangerous play was called the wedge play. Players would form a V around the player holding the ball. The offense would then run with the ball carrier in this position to protect him and lead him into the end-zone. As you can imagine, the mass and force of this large group of men charging toward the end zone resulted in many injuries. By 1905, there were eighteen deaths attributed to this violent game. Football was on its way to becoming extinct unless the rules were changed to make it safer.

Olympic Gold Medalist Jim Thorpe

FUN FACT

Jim Thorpe, winner of two gold medals in the 1912 Olympics (decathlon and pentathlon) was considered the greatest athlete of his day. Thorpe played pro football for the Canton Bulldogs in 1915, earning a whopping $250 per game and drawing significant attention to the game. Later, while still a player in the league, Thorpe was named the first commissioner of the NFL.

The most important rule change came in 1906 when the forward pass became a legal part of the game. The pass made the game more exciting and resulted in fewer massive pile-ups and therefore fewer injuries. Another significant change was requiring that seven offensive players had to be on the **line of scrimmage** at the beginning of each play.

In 1920, a group met to establish a full-time professional league called the American Professional Football Association (APFA). Two years later, the APFA became more organized and changed its name to the National Football League (NFL). With these and other important changes, football's popularity grew.

"Slingin" Sammy Baugh

FUN FACT

The Chicago Cubs major league baseball team was so popular in the Windy City that Chicago's professional football team changed its name from the Chicago Staleys to the Chicago Bears in hopes of gaining support from fans by using a similar team name.

From the 1930's to the 1950's, football gained a larger following due to exploits of athletes like Sammy Baugh and Sid Luckman. In 1937, "Slingin" Sammy Baugh began his hall of fame football career playing offense, defense, and special teams for the Washington Redskins. Baugh played for sixteen years and set records that still stand today, in passing, punting, and interceptions. Luckman, a hall of fame quarterback who played for the Chicago Bears for twelve seasons beginning in 1939, led his team to four NFL championships, beating the Redskins by 73-0 in one championship match-up. Luckman was the first NFL quarterback to throw seven touchdown passes in one game.

Sid Luckman

In the 1950's the game of football benefited from the glamour of players like Frank Gifford, an all pro running back who is now enshrined in football's Hall of Fame. After his playing career, Gifford became a sports broadcaster on *Monday Night Football*. Gifford is the husband of Kathie Lee Gifford, of *Regis and Kathie Lee* fame.

Frank Gifford

The upstart AFL...

In 1960, Dallas businessman Lamar Hunt established the American Football league (AFL) as a direct competitor to the NFL. Many other leagues had tried to compete, but it wasn't until the AFL that the NFL had a real competitor.

The AFL offered higher salaries to incoming talent, and many college stars (such as "Broadway" Joe Namath) turned down the NFL to play for the AFL. The rivalry was positive, however. The two leagues competed for television exposure and draft picks, drawing attention to the sport. At first the NFL completely ignored the AFL, assuming that the upstart league wasn't good enough to warrant attention. Eventually, both leagues agreed that a merger was in the best interests of the game. By 1970, the year in which the merger was officially complete, football had gained much fanfare and attention around the United States.

Vince Lombardi

FUN FACT

Legendary coach Vince Lombardi (Green Bay Packers, 1959 to 1968; Washington Redskins, 1969), is known as one of the toughest and most focused coaches who ever led a team. A quote commonly attributed to Lombardi, "Winning isn't everything. It's the only thing," is one of the most quoted lines in sports. His Packers won the first two Super Bowls in 1967 and 1968.

HELPFUL HINT

A team has a head coach and numerous assistant coaches with specialties such as offense, defense or special teams.

The Super Bowl...

In 1967, the AFL and NFL agreed to hold a post-season championship game with the winner of the AFL pitted against the winner of the NFL. This annual event came to be known as the Super Bowl. Football seemed tailor-made for the television era, and TV helped to greatly increase football's popularity. Football, with all of its intricate plays, offered more excitement than a radio announcer could capture.

In 1970, the ABC network made a risky decision to show a thirteen game Monday night football schedule. The gamble paid off, as ABC's *Monday Night Football* became a hit. Twenty-six years later, the show is one of the longest running series on television, in a class with *The Wonderful World of Disney* and *60 Minutes*.

In the early years of the AFL, it was widely believed that the NFL teams were superior to the AFL teams. But in 1969 at the third Super Bowl event, the AFL, thanks to Joe Namath and the New York Jets, proved everyone wrong with a surprise victory.

One league again...

The AFL and NFL officially merged in 1970 into two distinct conferences under the NFL name. The two conferences were now called the American Football Conference (AFC) and National Football Conference (NFC).

Joe Namath

> # FUN FACT
>
> Joe Namath, also known as Broadway Joe, played quarterback for the New York Jets from 1965 to 1976 and for the Los Angeles Rams in 1977. The 1968-1969 Jets were slated as the heavy underdogs against the Baltimore Colts, who were led by passing leader Johnny Unitas and were considered "shoe ins" for the championship. Namath, in a brash show of confidence, guaranteed before the Super Bowl that he would lead the Jets to victory. Namath and the Jets pulled out a surprise victory beating the Colts 16 to 7. The Jets' victory gave the upstart AFL legitimacy as a competitor.

The rivalry between the NFC and AFC continues to this date, with an active debate over the strengths and weaknesses of each conference. In recent years the NFC has reigned supreme, with NFC teams winning twelve of the last thirteen Super Bowls. However, as with any sport, things can change quickly....and they certainly do change in football.

Johnny Unitas

> # FUN FACT
>
> Super Bowl XXX (in January, 1996) was broadcast to over 175 countries around the world, with over 750 million people watching the game. U.S. advertisers now pay over a million dollars for a 30 second commercial during the Super Bowl.

Remember...

- Football grew out of the sports of rugby and soccer.

- In 1920, a professional football league was established. In 1922, its name became the National Football League (NFL).

- The Super Bowl is a championship game between the American Football Conference (AFC) and the National Football Conference (NFC). •

11

WATCHING AND ENJOYING THE GAME

Now that you know so much about the game of football, it's worth spending a few minutes on how to enjoy the game and continue your learning.

It's up to you...

How to watch the game is largely up to you. As a fan, you don't have to understand all the intricacies that coaches and players have to memorize. Fans don't have to memorize anything. There won't be a quiz, and you can't get cut from the team. Watching a game should be enjoyable. And the more you learn about the game, the more you'll appreciate it. In fact, without much effort you can feel like you've been watching the game for years.

Listen for the lingo...

Listen to the self-proclaimed football expert (we'll call him Joe Football) who will invariably be sitting next to you. You may or may not learn much about the game, but you'll pick up the colorful lingo of football. Of course you can choose, for your own use, to cut out the expletives.

Follow a team...

Follow the game on a regular basis and keep up with a favorite team or two and some favorite players. Watch an occasional Sunday afternoon match-up with friends. Once in a while, turn off *Melrose Place* to watch *Monday Night Football* (if you're an addict, you can tape *Melrose* for later viewing). Once you get hooked on professional football, you'll see

John Elway

how much fun you can have. The trials and tribulations of your favorite players, on and off the field, can rival any soap opera for drama, suspense, and sometimes humor.

Learn from the TV commentators...

Pay attention to the network commentators. Some have been hired for their ability to explain the game effectively. Others are known for their colorful, entertaining commentary. Watching on TV, you'll hear play-by-play analysis and see instant replays on key plays. Much of the discussion in a typical game is devoted to educating the home viewer about this complex sport.

See it in person...

Go to a game. Watching the game live at the stadium is much different than watching on TV. You won't be limited to the highlights the camera crew wants you to see. There are many behind-the-scenes battles that are pretty intriguing if you know where to look. Also, being with other fans is infectious. But, don't wear your favorite clothes, because sometimes fans get overly enthusiastic and there are a lot of things to spill at a football game.

Follow the ball...

Follow the progression of the ball down the field, and test yourself on plays to see if you can predict what will happen next. Watch the ball. This is not as easy as it sounds in a fast moving game, and even experts get fooled sometimes. Here are some helpful guidelines to get you started:

Keep your eye on the quarterback as he takes the snap from the center. When the quarterback gets the ball, watch his movement and you should know in a few seconds whether it is likely to be a running play or a passing play.

Watch the quarterback on running plays...

On a **running play**, the quarterback will usually hand the ball off to a running back who comes from behind him to take the ball. The offensive linemen are charged with opening up an area on the field for the running back to run through so he can move the ball downfield. Sometimes the quarterback will fake the handoff, dropping back to throw the ball to one of his eligible receivers. This is often called a **play action pass,** and a good one will often fool the crowd or even the TV cameraman.

A run up the middle is sometimes called a **draw play,** and a run around the end of the line is sometimes called a **sweep.**

Sometimes the quarterback will keep the ball and run it himself. In short yardage situations, with one to two yards or less needed for a first down, the quarterback may quickly plunge over the line of scrimmage, behind a lineman, on a play called a **quarterback sneak.**

And on passing plays...

If the quarterback takes the ball, takes several steps backwards, and looks downfield, you're probably going to see a **passing play**. Passing plays often make for exciting football because there is the opportunity to gain significant yardage and the risk of losing the ball to an interception.

The area on the field where the quarterback **drops back** for a pass is known as the **pocket.**

Watch the offensive linemen...

If you don't want to always focus on the quarterback, another way of determining whether the play will be a running play or **passing play** is to watch the offensive linemen, particularly the guards.

On running plays, the guards will often surge forward aggressively to try to push back the defensive linemen and create running room for the player with the ball. However, the guards could be trying to fake out the

> ## HELPFUL HINT
>
> Watch John Madden (now a commentator for Fox) describe the game. Madden knows football inside and out and is funny too. He uses modern technology to diagram his interpretation of a particular play on the screen. His marks go all over. You'll sometimes even find him drawing diagrams around fans in the stands or tailgaters drinking beer in the parking lot. Madden, who saw his pro career end with a knee injury in his rookie season with the Philadelphia Eagles in 1959, went on to coach the Oakland Raiders to seven division titles between 1969 and 1978. Madden is colorful in his personal life as well. He refuses to fly in airplanes, so he travels around the country in specially outfitted buses.

Neil O'Donnell, now quarterback for the New York Jets, winding up to throw a pass.

defense to make it look like a running play in the case of a **play action fake.**

FUN FACT

In 1906, the forward pass became legal. This important rule change occurred in part due to the dangerous nature of the game in its original form, before pads and modern plastic helmets.

If the guards drop back off the line of scrimmage, look for a passing play. If the guards step back, they are probably focusing on protecting the quarterback from oncoming rushers and giving him extra time to find a receiver.

Other factors that influence play selection...

A number of elements influence whether the offense will use a running play or a passing play on the next down.

Time remaining...

If there is limited time left before the end of the first half or the game, the team that is behind will often use more passing plays. In this situation, the team with the ball tries to preserve time on the clock. A completed pass typically results in more yards than an average running play. Passes also can move the ball near the sidelines where the

Barry Switzer

FUN FACT

In 1995, Dallas Cowboys' head coach Barry Switzer made an unusual and controversial call which is still criticized, even though his team went on to win the Super Bowl that season. In a division game against the Philadelphia Eagles late in the season, the score was tied with two minutes to go in the game. The Cowboys faced a fourth and one situation from their own 29-yard line. Instead of punting the ball downfield away from the Dallas goal line, Switzer kept his quarterback in the game and tried for a first down. When Dallas came up short of the required one yard, Philadelphia took over the ball deep in Dallas territory and kicked a field goal to win the game. Critics say that Switzer should have called for a punt, given his team's poor field position.

FUN FACT

Troy Aikman, in only his eighth season as quarterback for the Dallas Cowboys, has already led his team to three Super Bowl victories. The Cowboys were victorious over Pittsburgh in 1996 (Super Bowl XXX), and over Buffalo in 1994 (XXVIII) and 1993 (XXVII). Aikman was the Cowboy's first round draft pick out of UCLA in 1989. Only two other quarterbacks have more Super Bowl wins in their careers: Terry Bradshaw, who led the Pittsburgh Steelers to four NFL championships between 1975 and 1980 and Joe Montana who led the San Francisco 49ers to four NFL championships between 1982 and 1990.

Troy Aikman

receivers are in a better position to run out of bounds and stop the clock. Also, you may recall that the game clock stops after an incomplete pass.

On the flip side, if a team has a lead its coach might find it in the team's best interest to run out the clock and therefore he may call more running plays. Running uses more time on the clock and exposes the offense to less risk of a turnover.

What down is it and what yardage is needed?...

As you have learned, the offense faces differing decisions depending on the down and distance needed for a first down. The offense is most likely to pass on later downs when there is more yardage needed. For example, third and ten is considered a passing down because the probability of gaining ten yards is greater on a passing play. Third and one is typically considered a running down because it is usually not very hard for the offense to gain one yard on a running play.

Steve Young

Watch the star players on each team...

Sometimes a major factor in the selection of a running or passing play is simply who are the stars of the offensive and defensive teams. For example, the 49ers have one of the best quarterback-wide receiver combinations in Steve Young and Jerry Rice. It's not too tough to guess that they

Jerry Rice

Emmitt Smith

probably have a pretty active passing game. The Cowboys, with world-class running back Emmitt Smith, will use a large number of running plays.

Nobody's perfect...

Don't worry if you can't anticipate every play correctly. Nobody can, not even the pros. That's part of what makes football so interesting.

Remember:

- Watch and listen to pick up the subtleties of the game.

- Keep your eye on the direction of the quarterback to see if he's likely to hand the ball to a player for a run or throw the ball to a receiver for a pass play.

- Watch the guards. Are they surging forward aggressively to block for a runner or are they stepping back to protect the quarterback?

- Pay attention to the time on the game clock and the down being played.

- Know the stars on a team so you know what tools each coach has at his disposal.

"Crazylegs" Hirsch pictured with his wife and son.

FUN FACTS

Some fans take their football a little too seriously. In 1954, when "Crazylegs" Hirsch of the Los Angeles Rams played what his fans thought was his last game, 500 swarming fans charged the field and tore his clothes off in search of souvenirs. On the other end of the spectrum, New York Giants fans were so distraught about their team's poor performance in 1978 that they built a bonfire with their season tickets on one Sunday afternoon. •

12

THE DRAFT

Draft day...

It's the middle of April, and football season should be long over. After all, wasn't it just a couple of months ago that you were watching the Super Bowl?

Well, get ready for the start of a new season of football hype surrounding the NFL **college draft.** Draft day is when pro teams select from the top college prospects. This is a day when lives change, fortunes are created, and teams are reborn. OK, this may seem overly dramatic, but all these things do happen.

The very first college draft occurred in 1936 at a time when professional football need-ed a boost in popularity. The draft was designed to bring more competition and fairness to the teams in the professional league. The teams that fared the worst in the previous season were allowed to choose first from the new batch of young, fresh talent.

FUN FACT

It has become common to hear about multi-million dollar contracts offered to unproven draft selections who starred in college. But, it wasn't always this way. Football started off as an amateur sport. In 1892, professional football was born when William "Pudge" Heffelfinger (formerly an offensive guard at Yale) was offered $500 plus $25 for expenses to play for the Allegheny Athletic Association in a game against its rival the Pittsburgh Athletic Club.

The players...

Each year, before the draft, the sports press brings us stories of college stars with a shot at making it big in pro football. Some grew up poor in tough neighborhoods, dreaming of one day making it to the pros, while others are from comfortable suburbs. Some were highly sought after out of high school and got full scholarships, while others got no scholarships at all and defied the odds to make their teams as **walk-ons.** Some attended major colleges with established football programs, while others excelled at schools where football is considered unimportant. When the draft begins, however, all that matters is talent.

Coaches and team scouts put considerable thought and analysis into preparing for the draft. They attend games, watch game films, and furiously pour over statistics and scouting reports to try to identify potential stars. Most of the time this in-depth talent analysis helps them choose the right mix to suit their team's needs. However, coaches often mistake showmanship at major college events for raw talent, at times overlooking better players at smaller, lesser known schools.

Dan Marino signs a three-year contract worth $17.7 million. Marino is pictured here in April, 1996 with new Dolphins coach Jimmy Johnson.

FUN FACT

NFL teams don't always choose well in the college draft. For instance, future hall-of-famer (and all-time NFL passing leader) Dan Marino was not even selected in the draft's first round.
Five teams selected quarterbacks ahead of Marino, who was the 27th player selected when he graduated from Pittsburgh in 1983.

The nation's top college seniors, and in some cases undergraduates leaving college early, enter the NFL draft to make themselves available for selection. When draft day arrives and the names are called out in the first round of the draft, there is little that can match this thrill for college players. These young athletes will soon be facing their heroes, whose posters still line the walls of their college dorms, in head to head competition. They also face the prospect of once unimaginable wealth and fame.

The rules of the draft...

The draft has seven rounds, with each team getting one selection per round. Teams choose in order in each round, from the team with the worst record choosing first and the team with the best record choosing last.

Each team will try and choose the best player available at the time of selection. The best pick is not necessarily the most celebrated player, but one that can effectively fill a particular position on that team.

A player selected in the draft is required to play for the team that drafted him for a minimum of three years, after which time he is eligible to become a free agent. At the expiration of his contract a **free agent** can make a deal with any team that wants him.

Special expansion drafts...

In years in which the NFL adds one or more franchises, the league holds a special draft called an **expansion draft.** In 1995, the NFL added two **expansion teams,** the Carolina Panthers and the Jacksonville Jaguars. Thus, there was an additional expansion draft in 1995 to recruit players for these teams.

In an expansion draft, each team is allowed to protect (keep) a limited number of its players. Many team members are left unprotected and are at the risk of being drafted by an expansion team.

The success of Carolina and Jacksonville in building teams from players selected in the expansion draft, the college draft, and free agency led them to some surprisingly strong performances in the 1995-1996 season.

Remember:

- The draft is held on a day in late April, customarily in New York City.

- The draft is designed to help the weaker teams in the league improve.

- In each round, teams choose based on their prior season record, with the worst teams choosing first.

- There are seven rounds in the draft.

- A drafted player can become a free agent after three years.

- When new teams enter the league, the NFL holds an expansion draft. •

HELPFUL HINT

Teams can trade draft picks among themselves the way they trade players. It is not unusual to hear of a future draft pick involved in a trade between two teams involving one or more veteran players. For example, the Buffalo Bills may decide during the season to trade a defensive lineman, who doesn't fit into the Bills' current strategy, for a first round pick in next year's draft from the Atlanta Falcons, who need a lineman now. In the next draft, the Bills would now have two draft picks in the first round (theirs and Atlanta's) while the Falcons would not have a selection until the second round of the draft.

13

An Interview with Super-Agent
LEIGH STEINBERG

Agents to the stars...

Few people know the ins and outs of football as well as agents, who provide a variety of important services to the players they represent. Primary responsibilities include negotiating contracts with NFL teams, attracting and coordinating sponsorship deals and managing a variety of business affairs. Leigh Steinberg is widely considered the country's leading sports attorney. Representing over 100 professional athletes including football, baseball, basketball and hockey players, his law firm, Steinberg & Moorad, maintains a client list which includes some of the most high profile names in the sports industry. NFL players such as Troy Aikman, Steve Young, Derrick Thomas, Ki-Jana Carter, Jim Harbaugh, Drew Bledsoe and Thurman Thomas are among this esteemed group.

From his seat as advisor to the stars, top player agent Steinberg provides insight on the draft and NFL contracts, as well as personal anecdotes on his experiences as an agent in an exclusive interview.

Leigh Steinberg

Leigh Steinberg
speaks out...

BB: *Why did you decide to become an agent?*

LS: In 1971, I was living on campus at the University of California Berkeley as a graduate student counselor in an undergraduate dorm. Coincidentally, the football team was moved into this dorm. One of the students that moved in was Steve Bartkowski, who played quarterback at Cal. We became friends and after I graduated from law school in 1975, Steve approached me about representing him in the draft. As it turns out, he was the first pick of the draft that year (Atlanta Falcons).

I was stunned by the reaction Steve and I got when we arrived at the airport to sign him to his first contract with the Falcons. Television cameras swarmed us and lights were glaring when one television reporter said, "we interrupt the Johnny Carson show to give you a special news bulletin: Steve Bartkowski and his attorney, Leigh Steinberg have just arrived at the Atlanta airport, we switch you live to an interview." I looked at Steve like Dorothy looked at Toto and said, "I guess we're not in Kansas anymore". This idol worship gave me a very different perspective on athletes and athlete representation. I realized that if athletes utilize their high profile to serve as role models, they could utilize that profile in a positive way to make an impact in the world. I liked the idea of that.

BB: *What do you think about the college draft?*

LS: It is a common misconception that the draft was put into place to aid athletes. The draft actually exists to keep salaries down and to stop players from being free agents when they come out of college. Its ostensible rationale is that it creates parity in the league, but the true key to winning in football is the quality of the organization – the vision of the owner, the coaching ability of the coach, and the expertise of the front office. Good organizations still win, notwithstanding having the last pick in the draft – obviously having the last pick doesn't affect the Dallas Cowboys or the San Francisco 49ers.

BB: *How do teams decide whom to draft?*

LS: Each team has player personnel assigned to scouting the new players eligible for the draft. The teams send these scouts out in spring ball before their senior season.

When the regular season ends, scouting begins in earnest. There are elaborate scouting systems that dramatically affect where players are picked. The whole process starts with bowl games and the East-West Shrine game. The scouts go to these games and then grade these players on what's called triangle figures: size, strength, speed, athletic ability, agility and character. The players are given a one to ten point rating in each of these categories.

After this early process is complete, the players are summoned to an event called the scouting combine which is held in Indianapolis in early February. Every player attends and is weighed and measured — like a cattle call — is tested for drugs and external substances, goes through a physical, and then is tested in a number of different physical categories: the 40 yd. dash, the high jump, the vertical leap. Everything the athlete does during the Combine is videotaped.

When the combine is over, the scouts come back to the campuses and test again. Every player is given a Wonderlich test (a 40 question IQ test). There are also a variety of other tests that the athletes must endure, including hand speed for quarterbacks. Scouts also spend time in front of a chalk board to see how well the player can grasp basic football knowledge.

BB: *How do the athletes handle this process?*

LS: The whole process causes a lot of anxiety in these young athletes. One of the first things I do is counsel them on how to go through the process strategically. For example, Jeff George (starting quarterback for the Atlanta Falcons) is not the fastest guy in the league so we arranged that he would only have passing exhibitions.

BB: *What happens when a rookie player and his team have trouble reaching an agreement?*

LS: Being a holdout can be destructive for a rookie because the team's system of plays is sophisticated enough that he might not be able to catch up with the rest of the team. My job is to maximize their income, while giving them a normal playing career. Therefore, the trick is to get a player signed smoothly without

any public acrimony, negative newspaper stories or accusations.

We tell our players to go to camp even if they're not signed yet. My goal is to have a player show up and express himself in terms of community concerns, a public focus and a smiling face prior to training camp.

Before any players negotiate, we give a player an education on the world of contracts. In the end, he'll understand the economics of comparative contracts. The goal of successful representation is to empower an athlete to make his own decisions as opposed to spoon feeding him. We want the player to have power over his life.

BB: *How do you decide which athletes to represent?*

LS: When an athlete walks into my office for the first time, I ask him, what happens if you break your leg tomorrow? What other interests or talents do you have?

The profile of the athletes we represent is pretty distinct. We represent those that have a social conscience. An athlete has to learn how to prioritize and needs to ask himself, among other things: How important is family? Endorsements? How important is being on a winning team? How important is style of turf? In order to adequately represent them and fulfill their goals and needs, we need to really understand what they are made of. The average career span of a football player is 3.1 years. Therefore, we're talking of young men who have to transition into a second career at a very young age. A career can be terminated at any point — it's different from baseball and basketball, where the injury rate is not as high. With that said, I do my best to maximize the players' income, but more importantly I stress to athletes a sense of self-respect and being part of a nurturing environment — values that will stand the test of time. There is a real tendency for these players to be surrounded by external stimuli...newspapers, clippings, people who want to be around them because they're athletes. They're exposed to all sorts of material things. It's a rude awakening to an athlete when he realizes that these things are not around anymore. I always say, athletes die two deaths, one when they retire and one of natural causes.

BB: *Do these athletes really have good values? You hear more about the ones getting into trouble.*

LS: Anyone reading the paper gets a distorted view of athletes because the paper only talks of the aberrations. It's not news when an athlete wakes up in the morning, goes to the ball park, signs autographs, drives home safe and sober and sleeps with his wife.

It's not news when an athlete establishes a scholarship or when Troy Aikman (quarterback for the Dallas Cowboys) rebuilds part of Henrietta High School, repays his scholarship to UCLA and then, through the Aikman Foundation, endows a wing in a children's hospital in Dallas; or when Derrick Thomas of the Kansas City Chiefs launches a program that promotes children's literacy. Athletes have this

opportunity and many of them use it, but the media typically doesn't recognize these types of things as headline news.

BB: *How do you measure your success as an agent?*

LS: Part of my test to see if I have succeeded is to ask: Have I made them (the athletes) financially secure for life?

The economics of the sport have dramatically changed. Steve Bartkowski was signed in 1975 for a four year package totaling $600,000 dollars. That contract made headlines across the country as he (was to be paid more than) O.J. Simpson and Joe Namath. Last year I signed Ki-Jana Carter, the first round pick of the Cincinnati Bengals. While Steve received a signing bonus of $250,000 which made headlines everywhere, Ki-Jana Carter received a $7,125,000 signing bonus, which is cash up-front in his pocket.

The other measure of success is in financial planning, which is one of the crucial services we perform. These athletes don't know what to do with all of their money. So, we have people come in to teach them how to budget, what a long-term budget is, what taxes are, and how to avoid the pitfalls of other athletes. They've seen the horror of athletes who have come out of the sport with nothing. Because athletes are so revered, there are sophisticated financial planners who will represent athletes even if they don't make much. Almost all football players have been to college (four years and sometimes five, if they have to red shirt their first year in school); unfortunately, though, they haven't been schooled in dealing with financial planning.

BB: *What determines a "salary package"?*

LS: The signing bonus is the only part of the contract that is guaranteed cash up-front.

So if a player gets a total of $5,000,000 to sign and a salary of $1,000,000 for five years, then his overall package is reported as a five-year $10,000,000 deal.

Football is different in this respect from other sports. In basketball and baseball, most salaries are guaranteed, meaning that the team is committed to paying every last penny of the salary whether the player plays or not. Football, which has the highest level of injury, doesn't guarantee anything outside of the signing bonus. Everything else in the contract is at risk.

BB: *Can you provide an example of one of your more "innovative" contracts?*

LS: An example of one of our success stories is Drew Bledsoe's contract. (Bledsoe is the quarterback for the New England Patriots.)

I proposed a contract (for Drew) that focused on a new concept, which I brought to the forefront of negotiations in player contracts, called voidable years. What it says in simple terms is that if a player plays a certain percentage of plays in his first several years, then the last portion of his contract would disappear and (in Drew's case) after the first three years he would become a free agent.

After two years, it was clear that he would satisfy the percentage stipulations so the Patriots, instead of allowing him to play a third year and become a restricted free agent, renegotiated his contract in the summer of '95 and he received another $11.5 million in a signing bonus. Because the quarterback position is so powerful, the Patriots did not want to run the risk of losing Drew to free agency. Therefore, they were willing to renegotiate his contract. When all was said and done, he received $20 million in income in three years and $16,000,000 in signing bonuses alone, the most anyone has made.

BB: *This all sounds great, what's the negative side of being an agent?*

LS: I feel responsible for these players. The nasty secret is that most athletes leave pro football with some form of serious injury, some form of being disabled, and they live with that the rest of their life. In 1981 I had three top draft picks, each of whom left the game because of a disabling injury. These men, now in their 30's, will have to live the rest of their lives coping with those disabilities.

The most difficult thing to come to terms with is that football is not a healthy sport. The players are in a state of denial about the reality of their physical health. They are taught to play with pain; pain that would put you or me in bed for a week is something that they ignore.

Continued…

BB: *What is the most embarrassing thing that has ever happened to you in the business?*

LS: Most people have the perception of someone who signs athletes as being very slick; however, I usually cure people of that notion. I remember when I was signing a player in Kansas City a number of years ago. It was right before a press conference and I had just gained a fair amount of weight. When I leaned over in the general manager's office I heard a ripping sound. I stood there prior to this press conference in my underwear, with the secretary sewing my suit pants back on. It was very embarrassing.

BB: *Why do you think more women don't follow pro football?*

LS: It's just a matter of getting into it. For women, or even men who didn't grow up playing football, it's difficult to gain an appreciation and understanding of the intricacies and challenges involved in playing the game. With a better understanding of the rules, not to mention the hard work and camaraderie involved in football, I'm sure more women would learn to enjoy the game. Also, the game means much more to them if there is a human element that they can follow. Once they have a sense of who the players are and what the issues are, football becomes much more fascinating. •

14

THE PRE-SEASON

How the NFL is organized...

The National Football League (NFL) is made up of 30 teams. The number of teams increases over time, as new teams, called **expansion teams** because they expand the size of the league, are admitted. As you may remember, the NFL is divided into two divisions, the National Football Conference (NFC) and the American Football Conference (AFC). The AFC was originally made up of teams from the old American Football League, which merged with the NFL in 1970. The NFC is primarily made up of teams from the old NFL. Of course, each conference has been expanded over the years with expansion teams, which are highly sought after by cities. The newest expansion teams for the 1995-1996 season were the Jacksonville Jaguars and the Carolina Panthers.

Each conference is then divided into three divisions: Eastern, Central and Western. The use of divisions helps to bring order to the league and encourages regional rivalries. Teams in the same conference play each other twice a year and compete directly with each other for positions in the playoffs. The team in each division with the best win-loss record at the end of the season is assured a spot in the playoffs.

If you are a fan of the Miami Dolphins, who are in the AFC East division, you may be aware of that team's longstanding rivalries with the Buffalo Bills and the New York Jets. You may find yourself hoping that the Bills and the Jets lose games, even when they are not playing against the Dolphins, since a win by the Bills or Jets hurts the Dolphins' playoff prospects. See more on this subject in Chapter Fifteen, The Road to the Super Bowl.

Divisions were originally based on the geographic regions where the teams were located. The logic of this structure was, in part, to ease the travel burden on teams and players

┌─ ─ ─ ─ ─ ─┐

HELPFUL
HINT

It's probably not a good idea to root for two or more teams from the same division. Teams in the same division play each other frequently and often are fierce rivals. For example, try and avoid rooting for both the New York Giants and the Dallas Cowboys because they are in the same division (NFC East). It's much safer to be a fan of the New York Giants and an AFC team such as the Miami Dolphins.

└─ ─ ─ ─ ─ ─┘

during the season. However, as the league has expanded and franchises have moved around, the divisions have taken on some odd mixtures. For example, the Atlanta Falcons are in the NFC's West division.

The National Football League (NFL)

NFC	AFC
East	East
Central	Central
West	West

Training camp...

Preparation for the coming season starts after the April college draft. (See Chapter Twelve, The Draft.) Each team sets up training camp to prepare its players physically and mentally for the coming season. The first stage of a team's training camp, typically called **"mini-camp"**, is for the team's **rookies** (first year players). Soon after mini-camp, typically in early- to mid- July, the rest of the team reports to training camp where the players begin the process of getting their bodies back in shape. The coaches, who have spent countless hours prior to pre-season devising new plays and planning new strategies to combat the team's opponents, drill these new ideas into the players' minds.

Pre-season match-ups...

At the beginning of August, the official NFL pre-season starts. Each team plays four practice games against other teams in the league. However, the outcome does not count towards anything like it does in the regular season (a playoff spot), so the teams are playing for pride and for practice.

For the most part, coaches do not focus as much on the scores of the pre-season games as on the performance of the various squads and the individual players. Coaches use the pre-season to experiment with new plays and try out various players at different positions. A player whose spot on a team is in doubt will try extra hard to prove himself in the pre-season so as to earn a place on the team for the regular season. Coaches often limit the playing time of veteran players so as to reduce the risk of injury in a practice game. The pre-season is like a cross between an audition and a dress rehearsal for a Broadway show.

A Lott of pain...

Football players train hard during the pre-season and during the regular season, both physically and mentally. The best players keep themselves in prime physical shape during the off-season, but even these players turn their training up a notch when they get to training camp. Each veteran player, no matter how good, knows that there are rookies, younger and sometimes stronger, wanting nothing more in life than to beat him out of his position. By training hard during the pre-season and into the regular season, players are better prepared, mentally and physically, for games.

Ronnie Lott (star defensive back for the 49ers and later for the Raiders, Jets, and Chiefs) was known for his hard hitting and consistently high level of performance. Lott explained, for this book, the secret of his preparation for a game. During his career, he trained hard for a game and focused intently on one goal - that of beating his opponents. By game day, he would tell himself "I am prepared to give 110% for the people I respect — my family and my friends." And then he would go out and intimidate his opponents and contribute to his team.

Lott constantly pushed himself to the limit to train for the season, and as a result was named to Pro Bowl teams a remarkable ten times. He once chose, so as not to miss a single game, to have part of an injured finger amputated instead of having surgery which might have saved the finger. Lott described the intensity of preparing for games as both a physical and mental exercise. "When we prepare for games, it is painful. We agonize over every possible thing that could go wrong during a game."   •

Read more about training in Chapter Nine, A Week in the Life of a Professional Player.

Ronnie Lott
Defensive Back
San Fransico 49ers
Los Angeles Raiders
New York Jets &
Kansas City Chiefs

15

THE ROAD TO THE SUPER BOWL

No matter how much money, gold, and fame a player has, there's one piece of jewelry he can't buy. The Super Bowl ring, worn by players on an NFL championship team, must be earned.

A team's regular season in pro football has one aim – earning a spot in the playoffs, the first step towards going to the Super Bowl with a chance at becoming the next championship team. At the beginning of a season, 30 teams start out the season with an equal shot at the game's biggest prize, but only one will be left standing when the final game clock expires. This chapter is about how that team gets to call itself champion.

FUN FACT

The length of the NFL regular season has been expanding over time to reflect the addition of new teams and the insatiable appetite of pro football fans for more games. The sixteen-game regular season has been the norm since 1978. Before that, teams played a fourteen-game season from 1960 to 1977 and twelve-game season from 1947 to 1959.

From September through December – the regular season...

Each of the 30 teams will play sixteen games during the regular season. Teams will play one game a week, usually on Sunday, with one or two weeks off during the season.

Sixteen games might not seem like many compared to baseball or basketball, but the level of physical contact is much higher in football. Players generally find it takes the better part of a week to recover from a game and get ready for the next one (see Chapter Nine, A Week in the Life of a Professional Player). By the end of a sixteen week schedule, a large number of players on any given team have been sidelined with injuries.

"Broadway" Joe Namath beat the Colts in 1969 after guaranteeing a victory for the underdog Jets.

FUN FACT

The first championship game between the AFL and the NFL, back in January 1967, was not called the Super Bowl at the time it was played. The owners were not sure that the game would catch on, so the now famous title was not used. The founder of the American Football League, Lamar Hunt (see Chapter Ten, The History of the NFL) apparently came up with the name Super Bowl when he saw his children playing with a rubber ball called a Super Ball™. The name Super Bowl caught on and, shortly after the New York Jets beat the Baltimore Colts in 1969, became the official name of pro football's championship game.

Each team will play against the teams in its division twice, (once on its home field and once on the other team's home field). It will also play against a variety of other teams in the league based on a complicated formula, but not exclusively based on the team's division or conference.

The team with the best record in each division at the end of the regular season (the **division champion**) wins the division race and earns a playoff spot. The rest of the team has to compete for a limited number of additional positions. Teams that do not make it into the playoffs see their season come to a disappointing halt at the end of the regular season. For these players, the only way they will see a playoff game or the Super Bowl is on television or in the stands.

December into January — the playoffs...

After the completion of the sixteen game regular season, twelve teams earn the right to compete in the playoffs. The playoffs, together with the Super Bowl, are also known as the **post-season.**

A team can be guaranteed a spot in the playoffs by winning its division (having the best win-loss record in its division at the end of the regular season). Division champions account for six of the twelve available spots, three in the AFC and three in the NFC.

There are another six teams (three from the AFC and three from the NFC) that go to the playoffs without winning a division title. These **wild card teams** earn the right to compete in the playoffs based on having the best regular season win/loss records of all the teams that did not win division championships (see Time Out example in this chapter). The AFC and the NFC will each have three wild card teams. In the case of a tie (matching win-loss records), the league has developed a complicated formula (more difficult to unscramble than a Rubik's Cube™) to determine which team gets the last wild card spot.

FUN FACT

The Dallas Cowboys beat the Pittsburgh Steelers 27-17 in Super Bowl XXX (in January, 1996) in front of 76,347 fans in Tempe, Arizona. The win marked the fifth Super Bowl victory for the Cowboys, who have been to the Super Bowl a record eight times in 30 years.

The playoff match-ups...

The wild card teams play during the first week of the playoff series. Since there are six wild card teams (three from each conference), the two wild card teams with the best records in each conference play each other, while the wild card team with the worst win/loss record plays the division champion with the worst record.

After the wild-card round, there are four teams left in each conference. Note that the two division champions with the best records get to skip a round. This is a reward for success during the regular season.

The four remaining teams play two more rounds, until there is only one team left in each conference. The post-season is a single elimination tournament – so in each game the season is over for the losing team. The AFC champion goes on to meet the champion of the NFC in the Super Bowl.

Helpful Hint

The rewards of a good regular season are reaped in the play-offs. The teams with the best regular season records enjoy such "extras" as home field advantage and a "bye" in the first round of play-offs. The teams with worse records must play on the road, against teams with better records.

Tom Landry coached the Dallas Cowboys to two Super Bowl victories in five Super Bowl appearances between the 1970 and 1978 seasons.

The Super Bowl...

Dallas running back Emmitt Smith celebrates the team's victory in Super Bowl XXX.

49ers quarterback Steve Young, voted most valuable player of Super Bowl XXIX, clutches the Vince Lombardi trophy.

Unless you've been shipwrecked on a deserted island for 30 years, you've probably seen at least part of a Super Bowl (even if it was as little as just making a guest appearance at a Super Bowl party). The Super Bowl is played in January, after a two week preparation period. Cities compete aggressively for the right to host Super Bowl games, which are numbered with Roman numerals signifying the years since the first game in 1967. Super Bowl XXX (30) was played January 28, 1996 in Tempe, Arizona. The Super Bowl has evolved over the years into a monstrous media event — rivaling a royal wedding for pomp and ceremony, and a lunar landing for worldwide attention.

Super Bowl mania begins two weeks before the game, when the AFC and NFC champions are decided in the conference championships. The next two weeks become a frenzy of hype, speculation, and anticipation which builds to a crescendo on Super Bowl Sunday.

The Super Bowl has become the country's biggest single sporting event of the year, and is always a spectacular show. Even when the game turns into a rout, there's always plenty to watch, from the celebrities in the stands, to the trademark half time extravaganza, to the new crop of commercials that compete to entertain the viewing public.

The Super Bowl is unmatched in professional sports for the wide range of emotion displayed on the faces of the players, coaches, and fans, ranging from elation and joy to frustration and despair. Unlike baseball or basketball, which each end their playoffs with a seven-game championship series, the NFL selects its champion in one winner-take-all contest.

Every player and coach in football dreams of winning the

Super Bowl. Some star players are the best in the game at their positions for years but never play in or win a Super Bowl. Many would gladly exchange their own individual records for a Super Bowl ring if they had the chance.

Hall of Fame quarterback Fran Tarkenton led the Vikings to the Super Bowl three times without winning the big game.

FUN FACT

Certain cities seem to be cursed when it comes to the Super Bowl. For example, Buffalo and Minnesota have been to the Super Bowl a combined seven times without a victory (Buffalo four times in 1991, 1992, 1993, and 1994 and Minnesota three times in 1974, 1975, and 1977).

TIME OUT:

Here's an example of how the AFC playoffs unfolded in the 1995-1996 NFL post-season.

Three AFC Teams won division championships:		Three AFC teams won enough games to qualify for wild card spots:	
East:	Buffalo (10 wins, 6 losses)	**East:**	Indianapolis (9 wins, 7 losses)
Central:	Pittsburgh (11 wins, 5 losses)	**East:**	Miami (9 wins, 7 losses)
West:	Kansas City (13 wins, 3 losses)	**West:**	San Diego (9 wins, 7 losses)

As you can see, the wild card teams are selected based on next best record, not based on which division they play in (note the two teams from the AFC East).

The AFC wild card playoff games:
Even though Buffalo won its division, it did not have as good a record as Pittsburgh

> Buffalo beat Miami (37-22)
> Indianapolis beat San Diego (35-20)

or Kansas City, so Buffalo had to play an extra playoff round against a wild card team.

The second round:
In the second round of the playoffs, the divisional champion with the best record plays the surviving team from the first round with the worst record. The other

> Pittsburgh beat Buffalo (40-21)
> Indianapolis beat Kansas City (10-7)

divisional champion plays the other surviving team from the wild card round. Now, there are four teams left in the AFC.

The conference championship:

> Pittsburgh beat Indianapolis (20-16)

The two winners of the second round are the last two AFC teams remaining in the playoffs. They play each other in the third round called the conference championship game. The winner is the AFC champion.

The AFC champion (Pittsburgh) plays the NFC champion (Dallas) in the Super Bowl.

The Super Bowl:
Dallas defeats Pittsburgh (27-17)

16

ILLUSTRATION OF PENALTIES

T this chapter illustrates several of the most common signals used by the officials to indicate a score or a penalty against one of the teams.

TOUCHDOWN
(6 points)
FIELD GOAL
(3 points)
EXTRA POINT
(I or 2 points)

SAFETY
If one team gets trapped in its own end zone with the ball, the opposing team scores two points.

FIRST DOWN

is the initial down in each series of downs.

TIME OUT

The clock is stopped for one minute and 50 seconds (only 40 seconds when there is two minutes or less left to play). Each team is allotted three time outs per half.

PERSONAL FOUL

These penalties are fifteen yards and, in some cases, loss of down or automatic first down. This sign is used in combination with an additional sign indicating the particular personal foul. Personal fouls are unsportsmanlike and can be dangerous.

HOLDING

Offensive holding is ten yards, defensive holding is five yards plus an automatic first down. Holding occurs when a player uses his hands to grab the body or uniform of an opponent who does not have the ball.

PENALTY REFUSED

The team who did not commit the infraction can choose to refuse the penalty.

INCOMPLETE PASS

An attempted pass was not caught.

MISSED FIELD GOAL

A field goal attempt was unsuccessful.

PLAY OVER

This is also a signal used to indicate that the play has ended.

OFFSIDES OR ENCROACHMENT

This five yard penalty occurs when a player's body is beyond the line of scrimmage when the ball is snapped or kicked or a player enters the neutral zone and makes contact with an opponent before the ball is snapped.

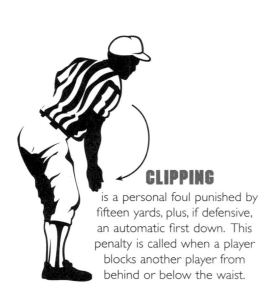

CLIPPING

is a personal foul punished by fifteen yards, plus, if defensive, an automatic first down. This penalty is called when a player blocks another player from behind or below the waist.

FACE MASK

penalty, if accidental, is five yards, if intentional, fifteen yards plus an automatic first down if against the defense. A face mask foul arises when a player grabs the face mask (plastic facial guard) of an opposing player's helmet during play.

17

THE CONFERENCES

NFC/AFC Teams-Profiles and Personalities

This chapter gives you a brief profile of the teams as of the beginning of the 1997-1998 season, organized by conference and division. Included are some unique historical facts and figures as well as the key players to watch out for. Don't feel like you need to read all of this, unless you want extra credit. Use it as a reference to learn about your favorite teams and their opponents. Please don't use this as your definitive guide however, because these descriptions are in summary form and players and coaches will change due to injuries, trades, and replacements.

Conferences and Divisions

NFC	AFC
NFC EAST	**AFC EAST**
Arizona Cardinals	Buffalo Bills
Dallas Cowboys	Indianapolis Colts
New York Giants	Miami Dolphins
Philadelphia Eagles	New England Patriots
Washington Redskins	New York Jets
NFC CENTRAL	**AFC CENTRAL**
Chicago Bears	Baltimore Ravens
Detroit Lions	Cincinnati Bengals
Green Bay Packers	Tennessee Oilers
Minnesota Vikings	Jacksonville Jaguars
Tampa Bay Buccaneers	Pittsburgh Steelers
NFC WEST	**AFC WEST**
Atlanta Falcons	Denver Broncos
Carolina Panthers	Kansas City Chiefs
New Orleans Saints	Oakland Raiders
St. Louis Rams	San Diego Chargers
San Francisco 49ers	Seattle Seahawks

NFC EAST

ARIZONA CARDINALS

- The Cardinals originally played in Chicago and then St. Louis. In 1988, the team moved to Phoenix.

- The Cardinals haven't had much luck since moving to Phoenix, and have yet to complete a winning (more wins than losses) season since moving to their new home.

TM

- Former coach Buddy Ryan (an aggressive and often tactless coach who once threw a punch at a fellow coach on his team) promised a Super Bowl spot and, having failed to deliver, was fired and replaced by Vince Tobin, formerly a defensive coach for the Colts.

Names to Remember: Coach - Vince Tobin
Quarterback - Kent Graham or
1997 draft pick Jake Plummer
Tight end - Chris Gedney
Wide receiver - Rob Moore

DALLAS COWBOYS

- The Cowboys are often called "America's Team" because of the team's broad support from fans across the country.

- The Cowboys have been a powerhouse for much of the last three decades, appearing in eight of 30 Super Bowls and winning five of them. Some legendary NFL figures were part of the winning Cowboy team, including quarterback Roger Staubach, running back Tony Dorsett, defensive end Ed "Too Tall" Jones and coach Tom Landry.

TM

- The Cowboys have again become a powerful force in the last few years. Super Bowl XXX in January, 1996 was the team's third in four seasons. Even with the many players who have left, due to free agency, Dallas still possesses an outstanding quarterback in Troy Aikman, running back in Emmitt Smith, and cornerback in Deion Sanders.

- The Cowboys' controversial owner, Jerry Jones, has not been shy about taking credit for his team's success. When the team was faltering, Jones replaced legend Tom Landry with Jimmy Johnson, who led the team to two Super Bowl victories. Jones then, to the surprise of many fans, fired Johnson and hired Oklahoma University's Barry Switzer, who coached the Cowboys in the 1995-1996 championship season.

Names to Remember: Coach - Barry Switzer
Quarterback - Troy Aikman
Running back - Emmitt Smith
Defensive back- Deion Sanders

NEW YORK GIANTS

- The Giants have seen many great players throughout their history. Among the greats are running back Frank Gifford, quarterback Y.A. Tittle, defensive tackle Rosey Grier, and defensive lineman Lawrence Taylor.

- The Giants won the Super Bowl in 1986 under the leadership of quarterback Phil Simms, who completed 22 of 25 passes in that game to beat the Denver Broncos.

- The team failed to live up to expectations in the last few seasons.

- The Giants are relying on new coach Jim Fassel (who replaced Dan Reeves) to improve upon the team's disappointing offense.

Names to Remember: Coach - Jim Fassel
Quarterback - Dave Brown
Running back - Tyrone Wheatley
Tight end - Howard Cross

PHILADELPHIA EAGLES

- The "Iggles" (as some Philadelphia fans call them) had successful seasons from 1947-9 and again from 1978 to 1981, but the team has never won a Super Bowl.

- Ray Rhodes, former defensive coordinator for the San Francisco 49ers, won the 1995 NFL coach of the year award in his first season as head coach of the Eagles for the team's 11-5 record. Rhodes is an intense coach that is known to open a jar of smelling salts when he needs an extra burst of energy.

- The Eagles have some fine talent in the running back combination of Ricky Watters and Charlie Garner who are known as "Thunder and Lightning".

- The Eagles will continue to rely on star wide receiver and ordained minister Irving Fryar as the premier target for quarterback Ty Detmer.

Names to Remember: Coach - Ray Rhodes
Quarterback - Ty Detmer
Running back - Ricky Watters
Wide receiver - Irving Fryar

WASHINGTON REDSKINS

- The Redskins had some great talent in the 1980's. With quarterback Joe Theismann, defensive end Dexter Manley, receivers Art Monk and Charlie Brown, and an offensive line (the "hogs"), the team was a perennial threat in the NFC conference.

- The last few seasons have been tough for this once power-ful team, which won a total of nine games in the 1994 and 1995 seasons combined.

- Coach Norv Turner believes post season play is a realistic possibility in 1997.

Names to Remember: Coach - Norv Turner
Quarterback - Gus Frerotte
Running back - Terry Allen
Tackle - Sean Gilbert

NFC CENTRAL

CHICAGO BEARS

- The Bears of old were known as the "Monsters of the Midway" because of their strong defense and powerful running.

- Over the years, the Bears have had some memorable players on the team, including Sid Luckman, Dick Butkus, Bronko Nagurski, Gale Sayers, and Walter Payton.

- Coach Mike Ditka led the team to a 15-1 regular season record and Super Bowl glory in 1985.

- In 1996 the Bears faltered to end the season at a disappointing 7-9.

Names to Remember: Coach - Dave Wannstedt
Quarterback - Rick Mirer
Wide receiver - Curtis Conway
Defensive end - Alonzo Spellman

DETROIT LIONS

- The Lions won three NFL championships in the pre-Super Bowl era of the 1950s, but then struggled for most of the 60s, 70s and 80s until 1989 when Heisman Trophy-winning running back Barry Sanders was drafted out of Oklahoma State.

- Sanders has been joined by 6'6" left-handed quarterback Scott Mitchell, who has elevated his game to become a powerful passer.

- With new coach, Bobby Ross (replacing Wayne Fontes), the team should improve in the 1997 season.

Names to Remember: Coach - Bobby Ross
Quarterback - Scott Mitchell
Running back - Barry Sanders
Wide receiver - Herman Moore

GREEN BAY PACKERS

- The Packers are still known for their two great dynasties, with Curly Lambeau, the team's coach and founder from 1929-44 and with Vince Lombardi, its coach from 1959-1967.

- Packer fans like to yell "the Pack is back", but they had little to yell about in the 1970s and 1980s. Now, "the Pack is back" with its impressive Super Bowl win in the 1996 season.

- Quarterback Brett Favre has developed into a superb passer and solid leader and the defense has one of the most formidable players at defensive end, Reggie White (the "Minister of Defense").

Names to Remember: Coach - Mike Holmgren
Quarterback - Brett Favre
Tight end - Mark Chmura
Defensive end - Reggie White

MINNESOTA VIKINGS

- Once known for the "purple people eaters" defensive line, the Vikings franchise boasts of the memories of star players like Fran Tarkenton, Joe Kapp, Rich Karlis, and Ahmad Rashad.

- The Vikings have traditionally been very strong contenders in the NFC Central division.

- Coach Dennis Green will rely on quarterback Brad Johnson (replacing injury-plagued Warren Moon) to lead the Vikings into a strong 1997 season.

Names to Remember: Coach - Dennis Green
Quarterback - Brad Johnson
Wide receiver - Chris Carter
Guard - Randall McDaniel

TAMPA BAY BUCCANEERS

- This relatively new franchise, which joined the NFL in 1976, has mostly struggled, with its highlight being 1979 when it won its division.

- In 1996, the Buccaneers hired their fourth head coach in seven years.

- The Buccaneers are relying on coach Tony Dungy, quarterback Trent Dilfer, and powerful linebacker Hardy Nickerson.

Names to Remember: Coach - Tony Dungy
Quarterback - Trent Dilfer
Middle linebacker - Hardy Nickerson
Running back - Warrick Dunn

NFC WEST

ATLANTA FALCONS

- The Falcons franchise has had some great players including quarterback Steve Bartkowski, receiver Andre Rison, kick returner Billy "White Shoes" Johnson, and defensive back Deion Sanders.

- 1997 marks the Falcon's 31st year in the league and, other than a few winning seasons and some scattered playoff berths, the team's performance has been somewhat frustrating to fans.

- Coming off a disappointing 1996 season, the Falcons hope their new coach Dan Reeves will make them playoff contenders.

- The team is counting on quarterback Chris Chandler and wide receiver Bert Emanuel to bring the Falcons a winning season.

TM

Names to Remember: Coach - Dan Reeves
Quarterback - Chris Chandler
Wide receiver - Bert Emanuel
Kicker - Morton Anderson

CAROLINA PANTHERS

- The Panthers are one of two expansion teams added in 1995 (the other is the Jacksonville Jaguars).

- For its first year of operation, the Panthers did better than most people expected, winning seven games. In 1996 the team surpassed expectations by winning the NFC West. The Panthers were one game away from going to the Super Bowl.

TM

- Carolina demonstrated a powerful defense led by its formidable core of linebackers.

Names to Remember: Coach - Dom Capers
Quarterback - Kerry Collins
Linebacker - Kevin Greene
Cornerback - Eric Davis

NEW ORLEANS SAINTS

- The Saints had such a disappointing start in the NFL that they were known as the "Aints".

- In 1986 the team's reputation changed and for the next six years the Saints started winning games in the NFC West.

- The Saints were led by quarterback Jim Everett, who previously played for the Los Angeles Rams, where he almost got into a fist fight with popular LA sportscaster Jim Rome. Everett charged Rome when Rome repeatedly called him "Chris" Everett on a cable television show.

TM

- After another disappointing season, the Saints hired "Iron" Mike Ditka (former coach of the Chicago Bears) to bring back some life to its faltering offense.

Names to Remember: Coach - Mike Ditka
Quarterback - Heath Shuler
Running back - Mario Bates
Defensive tackle - Wayne Martin

ST. LOUIS RAMS

- The Rams have had an unusual ride through NFL history. The team started in Cleveland in the late '30's and early 40's, then moved to Los Angeles in 1946 and stayed there until 1994, when they were moved to St. Louis. Georgia Frontiere (widow of Carroll Rosenbloom) is the current owner of the team and has the distinction of being the only female owner in NFL history.

- Ram stars over the years include Elroy "Crazylegs" Hirsch, Bob Waterfield, Lawrence McCutcheon, and Eric Dickerson. The Rams had an eventful offseason. They recruited Dick Vermeil (retired from coaching for the last 14 years) as the team's new head coach.

- The Rams traded up for the #1 pick in the 1997 draft to take the "pancake man" Orlando Pace.

- Isaac Bruce had a spectacular year in 1995 at wide receiver. He is called "The Reverend Ike" and hopes to be ordained as a minister.

Names to Remember: Coach - Dick Vermeil
Quarterback - Tony Banks
Wide receiver - Isaac Bruce
Offensive tackle - Orlando Pace

SAN FRANCISCO 49ERS

- The Niners are known as the team of the 1980's and could possibly become the team of the 90's. The era of coaches Bill Walsh and George Seifert with quarterback Joe Montana won four Super Bowl championships. When Steve Young took over quarterbacking duties in 1991, everyone thought that the 49ers heyday was over, but Young proved them wrong and has become one of the best quarterbacks in the league, leading the 49ers to yet another Super Bowl victory.

- The 49ers are known as a great passing team. Jerry Rice is generally considered the best wide receiver to ever play the game. He is the league's all-time leading touchdown scorer.

- The 49ers and the Dallas Cowboys are powerful rivals in the NFC conference, with one or the other going on to win the Super Bowl in six of the eight years between 1989 and 1996.

- The Niners shocked the football establishment by signing Steve Mariucci to replace George Seifert as head coach. Mariucci comes to San Francisco after one year of head coaching experience at the University of California.

Names to Remember: Coach - Steve Mariucci
Quarterback - Steve Young
Wide receiver - Jerry Rice
Safety - Merton Hanks

AFC EAST

BUFFALO BILLS

- The Bills have had stars who went on to become famous (Jack Kemp, former congressman, U.S. cabinet member, and Vice-Presidential nominee was the team's star quarterback in the 1960's) and infamous (O.J. Simpson was the team's star running back in the 1970s).

- Although the Bills' image suffers from the stigma of losing an unprecedented four consecutive Super Bowls between 1991 and 1994, they must be considered one of the strongest teams of the 1990s in the NFL.

- The Bills are aging but have some great veterans in running back Thurman Thomas and defensive lineman Bruce Smith.

TM

Names to Remember: Coach - Marv Levy
Quarterback - Todd Collins
Running back - Thurman Thomas
Defensive end - Bruce Smith

INDIANAPOLIS COLTS

- Formerly of Baltimore until 1984, the Colts have had some of football history's celebrated players, such as quarterback Johnny Unitas, fullback Alan Ameche, and defensive end Bubba Smith.

- The Baltimore Colts lost the infamous Super Bowl III to Joe Namath and the New York Jets.

- In 1994, the Colts' future brightened when they signed running back Marshall Faulk, who went on the receive Rookie of the Year honors in 1994.

TM

- In 1995, the team's future outlook improved further when Jim Harbaugh started at quarterback. He led the team to the 1995 AFC Championship game and within one play of making it into the Super Bowl. The 1996 season was somewhat of a disappointment, but if the team can remain healthy through 1997, they should have a rewarding season.

Names to Remember: Coach - Lindy Infante
Quarterback - Jim Harbaugh
Running back - Marshall Faulk
Wide receiver - Sean Dawkins

MIAMI DOLPHINS

- The Dolphins history is full of football legends including stars of the 1970s in quarterback Bob Griese, running back Larry Csonka, linebacker Nick Buoniconti, and kicker Garo Yepremian.

- In 1972, the Dolphins were the first team to complete a perfect NFL season, finishing 17-0.

- Current quarterback Dan Marino is considered one of the best NFL quarterbacks ever to play the game, having surpassed almost every passing record. However, Marino has never won a Super Bowl (the one major goal he has left in his outstanding football career).

- The controversial replacement of longtime coach Don Shula with former Dallas Cowboys coach Jimmy Johnson has Dolphin fans hopeful that Johnson can bring Marino and the Dolphins to Super Bowl success as he did with the Cowboys.

Names to Remember: Coach - Jimmy Johnson
Quarterback - Dan Marino
Running back - Karim Abdul-Jabbar
Wide reciever - O.J. McDuffie

NEW ENGLAND PATRIOTS

- The Patriots had been a relatively unexciting franchise until Bill Parcells (the former NY Giants coach, now the NY Jets head coach) took over as coach and Drew Bledsoe led the team to Super Bowl XXXI (1996 season).

- They now have a new coach, Pete Carroll, and a team anxious to go back to the "Big Game" and this time win it.

Names to Remember: Coach - Pete Carroll
Quarterback - Drew Bledsoe
Running back - Curtis Martin
Tight end - Ben Coates

NEW YORK JETS

- Jets fans will always remember Super Bowl III, when Joe Namath (see History of the NFL, Fun Fact) guaranteed a win for the heavy underdogs and then delivered. Unfortunately, that game was the only championship the Jets have won.

- The Jets have struggled through much of the 1970s, 1980s, and 1990s in the shadow of the Dolphins and the Bills, who have divided up most of the AFC east titles.

- After a 1-15 1996 season, the Jets hired Bill Parcells (away from New England) to try and turn the team around.

Names to Remember: Coach - Bill Parcells
Quarterback - Neil O'Donnell
Wide receiver - Keyshawn Johnson
Offensive tackle - Jumbo Elliott

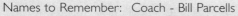

BALTIMORE RAVENS

- Until the end of the 1995-1996 season, this team was called the Cleveland Browns. Owner Art Modell moved the team from Cleveland to Baltimore, amid much controversy, agreeing to leave the Browns name behind.

- Baltimore fans, without a team since the Colts moved to Indianapolis, are thrilled to finally get another professional team.

Names to Remember: Coach - Ted Marchibroda
(ironically, the ex-coach of the Indianapolis Colts)
Quarterback - Vinny Testaverde
Wide receiver - Michael Jackson
(not to be confused with the singer)
Running back - Earnest Byner

CINCINNATI BENGALS

- The Bengals got off to a strong start in the late 1960s as an expansion team under legendary coach Paul Brown.

- The record since then has been mixed, with two Super Bowl appearances in 1982 and 1989, both losses to the 49ers.

- The team has struggled in the 1990s, but is making progress. The fans are optimistic about the team's chances under new coach Bruce Coslet.

Names to Remember: Coach - Bruce Coslet
Quarterback - Jeff Blake
Running back - Ki-Jana Carter (#1 draft pick in 1995)
Defensive end - Dan Wilkinson (#1 draft pick in 1994)

TENNESSEE OILERS

- The Oilers had three successful runs in their history, in the early 1960s, late 1970s, and late 1980s/early 1990s.

- The Oilers have had numerous playoff appearances over the years. However, the Oilers have never been to a Super Bowl.

- The Oilers lost their premier quarterback, Warren Moon, to the Minnesota Vikings in 1993. Steve McNair (the team's number one draft choice from 1995) should shine as the starting quarterback for 1997.

Names to Remember: Coach - Jeff Fisher
Quarterback - Steve McNair
Wide receiver - Chris "Tippy Toes" Sanders
Center - Mark Stepnoski

JACKSONVILLE JAGUARS

- 1995 was the Jaguars' first year as a team in the NFL and, to many observers, the team turned in a respectable performance for an expansion team, winning four games.

- The Jaguars, due to the new rules of free agency, lured many outstanding athletes out from under the arms of other teams. Equipped with enthusiastic players, the Jaguars came within one game in the 1996 season of appearing in its first Super Bowl.

Names to Remember: Coach - Tom Coughlin
Quarterback - Mark Brunell
Running back - Natrone Means
Offensive tackle - Tony Boselli

PITTSBURGH STEELERS

- In the early 1970's, the team was famous for its "steel curtain" defense with "Mean" Joe Greene on the defensive
line, Jack Lambert at middle linebacker, and quarterback
Terry Bradshaw and running back Franco Harris leading the
offense.

- Throughout the 70's the Steelers were devastating, becoming the first NFL team to win four Super Bowls.

- In 1996 (Super Bowl XXX), the AFC champion Steelers
were beaten by the Dallas Cowboys.

- However, the Steelers have been losing many free agents in the last couple of years.

Names to Remember: Coach - Bill Cowher
Quarterback - Kordell Stewart
Wide receiver - Yancey Thigpen
Running back - Jerome Bettis

DENVER BRONCOS

- If you take a trip out to Denver, you will see the team
color orange everywhere and John Elway auto dealerships
almost everywhere. Denver loves its Broncos, whose
defense used to be known as the "Orange Crush".

- The 1996 season was a disappointment to the Broncos.
With a star quarterback in John Elway and some of the
best players in the franchise's history, the team was devas-
tated not making it to the Super Bowl.

Names to Remember: Coach - Mike Shanahan
Quarterback - John Elway
Tight end - Shannon Sharpe
Linebacker - Bill Romanowski

KANSAS CITY CHIEFS

- The Kansas City Chiefs played in the first Super Bowl, losing to the Green Bay Packers.

- After winning a division championship in 1971, the Chiefs entered a seventeen year dry spell which lasted until the addition of coach Marty Schottenheimer, who, until the 1996 season, had made the team playoff contenders for six straight years.

- In 1993-1994, the Chiefs were led by former San Francisco star quarterback Joe Montana. Now the team has another solid quarterback in Elvis Grbac (another former quarterback from San Francisco).

Names to Remember: Coach - Marty Schottenheimer
Quarterback - Elvis Grbac
Running back - Marcus Allen
Tight end - Tony Gonzalez

OAKLAND RAIDERS

- The Raiders have had a proud history, winning Super Bowls in the 1976, 1980, and 1983 seasons. John Madden, now a well-known sportscaster, coached the Raiders to seven division titles and the team's first Super Bowl in his ten years.

- This team has moved from Oakland to Los Angeles and is now back in Oakland since the beginning of the 1995-1996 season. Oakland fans are ecstatic to have the "silver and black" team back.

- The Raiders are looking forward to some exciting plays by their new acquisition, Desmond Howard (Super Bowl XXXI MVP from the Green Bay Packers).

Names to Remember: Coach - Joe Bugel
Quarterback - Jeff George
Wide receiver - Tim Brown
Wide reciever - Desmond Howard

SAN DIEGO CHARGERS

- From 1979-82, the Chargers were known for their offensive power, yet they haven't been able to pull off enough big wins. The last couple of years have been similar. The Chargers made it to Super Bowl XXIX, but were crushed by the more experienced San Francisco 49ers.

- The Chargers have a new head coach in Kevin Gilbride (who replaced Bobby Ross).

- The Chargers are counting on many off-season changes to boost them to the playoffs. They are still, however, relying heavily on their quarterback Stan Humphries and all pro linebacker, Junior Seau (pronounced Say - ow, which is what he makes his opponents do).

> Names to Remember: Coach - Kevin Gilbride
> Quarterback - Stan Humphries
> Linebacker - Junior Seau
> Defensive end - William Fuller

SEATTLE SEAHAWKS

- The Seahawks were formed in 1976 as part of an expansion where the league also added the Tampa Bay Buccaners.

- The Seahawks had their most successful year in 1983, when Chuck Knox became the coach. The team featured quarterback Dave Krieg passing to Steve Largent who, was elected into the Hall of Fame and is still considered one of the Seahawks greatest players.

TM

- There was a big controversy after the 1995-1996 season, when the team's owner tried to move the Seahawks to Los Angeles. For now, the team will stay in Seattle.

- The Seahawks have one of the fastest receivers playing the game in Joey Galloway (who also graduated college with a business degree and a 3.2 GPA).

> Names to Remember: Coach - Dennis Erickson
> Quarterback - John Friesz
> Wide receiver - Joey Galloway
> Linebacker - Chad Brown

GLOSSARY

Note: Some of these definitions have been simplified for ease of use and may not include all possible scenarios which can conceivably arise in a game. Many terms and rules have been interpreted or adapted from the *1995 Official Playing Rules of the National Football League,* edited by Jerry Seeman, with permission of the NFL. For the official (and more technical) definitions, you can pick up a copy of the *Official Playing Rules* at your neighborhood bookstore.

ASTROTURF: A type of artificial turf; a synthetic carpet-like playing field surface used in some football stadiums to replace a natural grass playing field.

AUDIBLE: When the quarterback verbally signals to his teammates, at the line of scrimmage and before the snap of the ball, that he is changing the play from the one called in the huddle to another play. An audible is typically called in response to what the quarterback sees in the defense's formation.

BLITZ: When a player (or players) in addition to the defensive linemen rushes the quarterback to increase the probability of a sack.

BLOCKING: The term used when offensive players attempt to block, or push opposing players away from the quarterback or other ball carrier, using their bodies or limbs. Special teams players may also block on a kick return, and defensive players may block for a teammate who recovers a fumble or intercepts a pass.

BOUNDARY LINE: The white border surrounding all four sides of the field, including the side lines and the end lines, signifying the area out of the field of play.

CENTER: The player who lines up at the center of the offensive line and snaps the ball back to the quarterback to start the play.

CHAIN CREW: The three officials who keep track of the yardage and the downs on each play. Two officials are responsible for holding the ten-yard chain markers and one official holds the down marker.

CHAIN GANG: See chain crew.

CLIPPED: See clipping.

CLIPPING: An illegal block that occurs when a player throws his body across the back of an opponent's leg or hits the opponent [back] below the waist while moving up from behind (unless the opponent is a runner or the block occurs in close line play).

COLLEGE DRAFT: The process in which professional football teams select new players for their rosters from the top college prospects. This seven round event usually takes place in April.

CONVERSION: See extra point attempt.

CORNERBACK: A defender who lines up in the defensive backfield, in a corner of the defensive formation, with responsibility for covering offensive pass receivers. A defensive back. There are usually two cornerbacks playing defense at a time (see defensive backfield).

COUNT: See signals.

COVERING: The defense's tactic in guarding an offensive pass receiver to prevent the offense from completing a pass. A defender may run alongside the receiver and seek to deflect or intercept the ball, but may not make contact with the receiver until the receiver touches the ball (see defensive pass interference).

DEFENSE: The team that does not have possession of the ball at the beginning of the play and seeks to prevent the offense from advancing.

DEFENSIVE BACK-FIELD: The defensive players who play behind the linebackers in the backfield. The players in the defensive backfield are called defensive backs (cornerbacks and safeties).

DEFENSIVE END: A lineman who lines up on the end of the defensive line next to the tackles.

DEFENSIVE HOLD-ING: A penalty called on an defensive player when he tries to restrict the movement of a offensive player by grabbing on to that player's body or uniform.

DEFENSIVE LINEMAN: A defensive player (one of three or four on a given play) who starts the play on the line; there are two ends and one or two tackles depending on the particular defensive formation being used (see four-three, three-four formation). Defensive linemen rush the quarterback on passing plays.

DEFENSIVE OFF-SIDES: A penalty called on the defense when any part of a defensive player's body moves over the line of scrimmage before the ball is snapped and causes an offensive player directly opposite to react (move).

DEFENSIVE PASS INTERFERENCE: A penalty called when a defender interferes, by using physical contact, with an offensive receiver attempting to catch the ball.

DELAY OF GAME: A penalty called on the offense for taking longer than 40 seconds between plays.

DIVISION CHAMPION: The team in each division (east, central, or west in each conference) with the most wins at the end of the regular season.

DOWN: The period of action that starts when the ball is put in play and ends when the play is over.

DOWNING: When the ball carrier touches his knee to the ground in his own end zone thereby signaling a touchback.

DRAW PLAY: A type of delayed run up the middle by a running back which is made to appear to the defenders like a passing play.

DRIVE: A series of consecutive offensive plays by one team.

DROP BACK: When the quarterback takes a few steps back from the line of scrimmage in an attempt to pass.

ELIGIBLE RECEIVER: A player who is allowed to catch a forward pass, typically including receivers and running backs but not linemen.

ENCROACHMENT: When a player enters the neutral zone and makes contact with an opponent before the ball is snapped.

END LINE: The two parallel lines that represent the ends of the field. Each marks the end of an end zone, ten yards behind a goal line.

END ZONE: The area between the goal line and the end line which a ball carrier needs to enter in order to score a touchdown.

EXPANSION DRAFT: The supplemental draft (selection process) held to accommodate the formation of new teams in years when the NFL adds one or more franchises (expansion teams).

EXPANSION TEAM: A new team granted an NFL franchise, during its first season.

EXTRA POINT ATTEMPT: After a touchdown, the scoring team is allowed an extra point try during one scrimmage down. The ball may be spotted anywhere between the sidelines, two or more yards from the goal line. A successful attempt, or conversion, scores one point for a kick through the goal posts or two points for running or passing the ball over the goal line.

FACE MASK FOUL: A penalty that arises when a player grabs the face mask (plastic facial guard) of an opposing player's helmet during play.

FAIR CATCH: An unhindered catch of a kick by a member of the receiving team who signals his intention by raising one arm full length above his head and waving it from side to side while the kick is in flight. A player signaling a fair catch forfeits his eligibility to run with the ball.

FALSE START: A penalty called when the offense moves before the snap of the ball, regardless of whether that player actually crosses the line of scrimmage.

FIELD GOAL: When the offense kicks the ball from the playing field through its opponent's goal posts. If the ball goes through the goal posts, it is worth three points.

FIRST DOWN: The initial down in each series of downs is known as the first down.

FIRST DOWN MARKER: A vertical post carried by one of the officials on the chain crew. The post has a sign on top which displays the number of the down being played to the players and spectators.

FORWARD PASS: A pass thrown in the direction of the defensive goal line after leaving the passer's hands and before touching another player.

FOUL: Any violation of a playing rule.

FOUR-THREE, THREE-FOUR FORMATION: Two typical defensive formations reflecting the number of linemen and linebackers: The four-three describes four linemen (two tackles and two ends) and three linebackers while the three-four describes three linemen (one nose tackle and two ends) and four linebackers.

FREE AGENT: A player who, after three years in the league, is eligible to start negotiating with any team that wants him.

FREE KICK: A kickoff or kick after a safety. A free kick may be a placekick, dropkick or punt except a punt may not be used on a kickoff.

FULLBACK: A running back.

FUMBLE: The loss of possession of the ball when the carrier drops it or has it knocked out of his hands. A fumble can be recovered by either team. The recovering team starts the next play on offense.

GAME CLOCK: The clock on the scoreboard which keeps track of time remaining in each quarter. Each quarter is fifteen minutes long and halftime is twelve minutes. The time between plays is limited to 40 seconds from the end of one play to the beginning of the next play.

GOAL LINE: The line between the field of play and the end zone over which a team must move the ball to score a touchdown. The goal line is ten yards in from the end line.

GOAL POSTS: Two vertical posts connected by a crossbar, at each end of the field. The kicking team must kick the ball between the vertical posts and above the crossbar for a field goal or extra point conversion.

GRIDIRON: A term used to describe the football playing field.

GUARD: An offensive lineman, one of two who line up on each side of the center. A guard is responsible for blocking for the quarterback and running backs.

HALFBACK: A running back.

HAIL MARY: A long desperation pass.

HALFTIME: The intermission between the second and third quarters during which the two teams retreat to their respective locker rooms. Halftime now lasts twelve minutes.

HAND-OFF: When the quarterback hands the football to another player on offense (typically a running back) who will run with the ball.

HANG TIME: The amount of time that a punter's kick remains in the air. Normally, a longer hang time favors the punting team.

HASH MARKS: Two parallel sets of short markings on the playing surface, running the length of the field in line with the goal posts.

HUDDLE: The brief offensive and defensive meetings that occur on the field before the beginning of a play. In the huddle, each team learns its strategy for the next play.

ILLEGAL FORWARD PASS: A penalty when a forward pass is thrown from beyond the offense's line of scrimmage (a passer must remain behind the line of scrimmage when passing the ball).

INCIDENTAL CONTACT: Contact made between a receiver and a defender that does not negatively affect or significantly impede the receiver.

INELIGIBLE RECEIVER: An offensive player who may not touch or catch a forward pass, which may be caught only by an eligible receiver. Offensive linemen (center, guards, and tackles) are not eligible to receive passes unless a defensive player or an eligible receiver has already touched the ball.

INFRACTION: A penalty.

INTENTIONAL GROUNDING: A penalty called when a quarterback intentionally throws an incomplete pass — away from any intended receivers — to avoid being sacked for a loss of yardage.

INTERCEPTION: When a pass is caught by an opponent of the passer before it touches the ground.

KICK RETURN: When the receiving team takes possession of the ball which has been kicked and attempts to run it back towards the kicking team's goal line.

KICKING TEAM: A special team squad that is responsible for kicking the ball.

KICKOFF: The kick from a tee on the kicking team's 30-yard line at the start of each half and after a field goal or extra point attempt. A kickoff is a type of free kick. A kickoff is illegal unless it travels ten yards or is touched by the receiving team. Once the ball travels ten yards or is touched by the receiving team it is a live ball which can be recovered by either team.

LATE HIT: A penalty called when a player tackles or blocks an opponent after the play has clearly ended.

LATERAL: A backward or sideways pass. Unlike a forward pass, a lateral can be thrown more than one time during a play. A lateral which touches the ground is a live ball.

LINE OF SCRIMMAGE: An imaginary line where players line up at the start of each play. Players are not allowed to cross the line of scrimmage before the snap of the ball or they will be penalized.

LINEBACKER: One of the defensive players who line up behind the defensive linemen; there can be three or four linebackers depending on which defensive formation is used (see four-three, three-four).

LIVE BALL: A ball legally free-kicked or snapped, which continues in play until the down ends.

MAN TO MAN DEFENSE: A defensive formation in which defensive players cover specific opposing players rather than specific areas of the field.

MIDFIELD: The middle of the field, marked by the 50-yard line.

MINI-CAMP: Two- to five-day training sessions for players during the off-season.

MUFF: The touching of a loose ball by a player in an unsuccessful attempt to obtain possession.

NEUTRAL ZONE: The space the length of a ball at the line of scrimmage. The offensive team and defensive team must remain behind their ends of the ball. The sole exception is the center, the offensive player who snaps the ball.

OFFENSE: The team with possession of the ball at the beginning of the play, which seeks to advance the ball and to score points.

OFFENSIVE BACK-FIELD: The offensive players who start a play behind the offensive line. Usually consists of the quarterback and the running backs.

OFFENSIVE HOLD-ING: A penalty called on an offensive player when he tries to restrict the movement of a defensive player by grabbing on to the defender's body or uniform.

OFFENSIVE LINEMAN: One of the players on offense who line up along the line of scrimmage and block for the quarterback or running back.

OFFENSIVE OFF-SIDES: A penalty called when any part of an offensive player's body is beyond his line of scrimmage (or free kick line) before the ball is snapped or kicked.

OFFSIDES: A penalty called on a player when any part of his body is beyond his line of scrimmage (or free kick line) when the ball is snapped or kicked.

ONSIDE KICK: When a kicker tries to kick the football on a kickoff so that it bounces and goes just beyond the required ten yards.

OUT OF BOUNDS: When a player or the ball touches the ground outside of the boundary lines bordering the field.

OVERTIME: An extra period of play when the score is tied after the completion of four quarters. Also known as sudden death, overtime ends with the first score by either team.

PASS INTERFERENCE: A penalty called against the offense or defense when a player interferes with the opposing player's attempted catch by using physical contact while the ball is in the air.

PASS RECEIVER: An eligible offensive player who runs downfield in a effort to catch a forward pass.

PASS RUSH: When the defense crosses the line of scrimmage in an effort to sack the quarterback, block a pass, or otherwise interfere with his passing attempt.

PASSING PLAY: A play on which the offense seeks to complete a forward pass. Typically, the quarterback will take several steps back and look downfield to try and find an open receiver.

PASS PATTERN: The route that an offensive receiver runs when he is trying to get open on a passing play.

PENALTY: The punishment assessed against the team committing an infraction (rule violation). Depending on its seriousness, a penalty can cost the offending team anywhere from five to fifteen yards and a loss of a down. For the most serious violations, a player can be ejected from the game.

PERSONAL FOUL: Any infraction called for a penalty that might cause injury to a player.

PLACE KICK: A kick made by a kicker when the ball is on the ground, including a kickoff, a field goal, or an extra point attempt. A kickoff is typically kicked from a plastic holder (see tee). A field goal attempt or extra point attempt is held in place by a teammate of the kicker.

PLAY ACTION FAKE: See play action pass.

PLAY ACTION PASS: A trick play which looks like a running play (often with a fake hand-off) but is actually a passing play.

PLAYOFFS: The post season tournament which determines the winner in each conference (the AFC and NFC) who will play each other in the Super Bowl championship game.

POCKET: The area into which a quarterback steps back to attempt a pass.

POINT AFTER TOUCHDOWN: An attempt by a team that has just scored a touchdown to score an additional point.

POST-SEASON: The playoffs and the Super Bowl.

PUNT: A kick made when a player drops the ball behind the line of scrimmage and kicks it before it drops to the ground. A punt cannot be recovered by the punting team unless the ball is touched by the receiving team.

QB: Slang for quarterback.

QUARTERBACK: The leader of the offensive squad who calls and initiates plays. Also QB.

QUARTERBACK SNEAK: An attempt by the quarterback to quickly carry the ball up the middle (often by diving forward) to gain the short yardage necessary for a first down or touchdown.

RECEIVER: An offensive player who is eligible to catch a pass; an eligible receiver can include a wide receiver, running back, or tight end.

RECEIVING TEAM: The special team which receives kickoffs or punts.

ROOKIE: A player in the National Football League during his first season.

ROUGHING THE PASSER: A personal foul which occurs when a defender tackles or runs into the quarterback after the QB has already handed off or passed the ball away, unless the hit is unintentional.

RUNBACK: See kick return.

RUNNING BACK: One of the players on offense who line up behind the quarterback to run with the ball.

RUNNING PLAY: A play on which the offense attempts to advance the ball by carrying it forward. Often, the quarterback will hand the ball off to a running back who takes the ball and runs with it.

SACK: When a quarterback is tackled for a loss of yardage behind the line of scrimmage while attempting to pass the ball.

SAFETY: One of the defensive backs who line up in the defensive backfield and serve as the last line of defense. There are typically two safeties in a defensive formation; **or:** the scoring situation when a player with the ball is tackled on or behind his team's own goal line. A safety earns two points for the opposing team.

SECONDARY: See defensive backs

SET: The stationary crouching stance that all linemen must be in before the snap of the ball.

SIDELINES: The boundaries that run along the sides of the field marking the end of the field of play.

SIGNALS: The sign that an official makes with his hands, arms, and body to signify a particular penalty; Alternatively, a verbal code of numbers, letters and words that the quarterback uses to describe the next play.

SNAP: When the center picks up the ball to hand it back to the quarterback officially beginning the play.

SPEARING: A penalty called on a player for using his helmet to hurt his opponent.

SPECIAL TEAMS: The opposing squads of players who participate on kicking situations.

SPIRAL: When the ball is passed or kicked with a rotating side-ways spin that causes it to travel further downfield and with more accuracy. The football is shaped to be thrown in a spiral.

SPOT: The placement on the field of the ball where the previous play ended or where it is moved because of a penalty.

SPOTTING: See spot.

SQUIB KICK: A ball kicked downfield that is low and bouncing to make it more difficult to catch.

SQUIBBLER: See squib kick.

SUBSTITUTION: Each team is permitted eleven players on the field at one time. Unlimited substitution (replacement of players) is permitted between plays, but no substitution is allowed once a play has begun.

SUDDEN DEATH: The continuation of a tied game into overtime when the team scoring first (by field goal touchdown, or safety) wins. See overtime.

SUPER BOWL: The culmination of the regular season and the post season; the championship game between the winner of the AFC conference and the NFC conference takes place in late January at a predetermined neutral site.

SWEEP: An attempted running play by an offensive running back which goes wide (around the end of the offensive line, rather than through the center of the offensive line as on a draw play).

TACKLE: An offensive tackle is a lineman who lines up outside the offensive guards. A defensive tackle is a lineman who lines up inside the defensive ends. On offense there are two tackles and on defense there are one or two tackles (depending on the particular formation). A tackle is also a tactic used by a defender to bring the ball carrier to the ground.

TEE: A plastic holder on which the ball may be placed for a kickoff.

TIGHT END: An offensive player who lines up on the end of the line of scrimmage and has responsibilities which alternate between receiving passes and blocking.

TIME OUT: A chance for a team to regroup and plan its strategy. Each team is allotted three time outs per half.

TOUCHBACK: When a kick returner catches the ball in his own end zone and elects not to run it back out of the end zone, he signifies the election of a touchback by touching one knee down on the field. The next play automatically starts on the receiving team's 20-yard line. A touchback also occurs automatically when a kicker kicks the ball past the receiving team's end zone.

TOUCHDOWN: When any part of the ball, legally in possession of a player inside the sidelines, is on, above or over the opponent's goal line. A touchdown is worth six points to the scoring team.

TRY: See extra point attempt.

TURNOVER: The loss of possession of the ball to the opposing team during a play. Can occur as a result of a fumble or an interception.

TWO MINUTE WARNING: An announcement by the referee that there are two minutes left in the half or in the game. A time out is awarded which does not use one of either team's remaining time outs.

TWO POINT CONVERSION ATTEMPT: See extra point attempt.

UNNECESSARY ROUGHNESS: A penalty called for any action by a player that is deemed dangerous and unnecessary.

UNSPORTSMANLIKE CONDUCT: A penalty which results from any act committed by a player which is contrary to the generally understood principles of sportsmanship.

WALK-ON: A college player not recruited to play football or granted a football scholarship who nonetheless makes the team.

WIDE RECEIVER: A receiver who lines up outside the offensive tackle. An offensive configuration can use from one to three wide receivers, who are responsible for catching the majority of passes on offense.

WILD CARD TEAM: A team that does not win its division but has a good enough win/loss record to win a spot in the post-season playoffs. Three wild card teams from each conference (regardless of division) earn the right to compete in post-season play.

YARD LINES: Marks along the length of the field to keep track of each team's progress on the field.

ZONE DEFENSE: A type of defensive strategy that requires the defenders to cover specific areas of the field rather than specific players.

INDEX

NOTES

NOTES

ORDER FORM

The WOMEN'S
Armchair Guide to Pro
FOOTBALL

BETSY BERNS

To order by phone,
call **Toll Free:**

1-888-4-TOUCHDOWN
1-888-486-8243

or send this form to:

BVision Sportsmedia, L.P.
F.D.R. Station
P.O. Box 1176
New York, NY 10150-1176

Name:...

Street Address:...

City:...State: .... Zip: ....

Telephone: ....

❑ Please also enroll me as a charter member of the Women's Institute for Football Education (W.I.F.E.) with a free trial membership.

Sales Tax: Add $1.00 for books shipped to New York addresses.
Shipping: $3.50 per order.

Payment:
❑ **Check**   **Credit Card:** ❑ VISA   ❑ MasterCard   ❑ AMEX

Card Number:...Expiration Date: ....

Name on Card: ....

Signature:..

Call Toll Free and start enjoying football today!
1-888-4-TOUCHDOWN
1-888-486-8243

ORDER FORM

The WOMEN'S
Armchair Guide to Pro
FOOTBALL

BETSY BERNS

To order by phone,
call **Toll Free:**

1-888-4-TOUCHDOWN
1-888-486-8243

or send this form to:

BVision Sportsmedia, L.P.
F.D.R. Station
P.O. Box 1176
New York, NY 10150-1176

Name:..

Street Address:...

City:..State: .... Zip: ....

Telephone: ....

❑ Please also enroll me as a charter member of the Women's Institute for
Football Education (W.I.F.E.) with a free trial membership.

Sales Tax: Add $1.00 for books shipped to New York addresses.
Shipping: $3.50 per order.

Payment:
❑ **Check**   **Credit Card:** ❑ VISA   ❑ MasterCard   ❑ AMEX

Card Number:...Expiration Date: ....

Name on Card: ....

Signature:..

Call Toll Free and start enjoying football today!
1-888-4-TOUCHDOWN
1-888-486-8243